BOY ON A UNICYCLE

confessions of a
young man trained
to be a winner

dan mccall

edited by
steven mccall

Outpost19 | San Francisco
outpost19.com

Copyright 2017 by Steven McCall.
Published 2017 by Outpost19.
All rights reserved.

McCall, Dan
    Boy On A Unicycle: Confessions of A Young Man Trained To Be A Winner / Dan McCall
        ISBN: 9781944853334 (pbk)

Library of Congress Control Number: 2017906004

OUTPOST19

ORIGINAL
PROVOCATIVE
READING

Praise for
Boy on a Unicycle:
Confessions of a Young Man Trained to be a Winner

"*Boy on a Unicycle* is the powerful story of a heavily tutored show kid who sucked in unquestioning minds with a dramatically sentimental presentation of patriotism. It provides one hell of a peek behind the curtain of the saccharin image of WASP life promoted largely through TV sitcoms of the '50s... If there was something formally called WASP Studies, this book would be essential reading."

— Reuben Munday

"*Boy on a Unicycle* is a great book by a shamefully under-recognized American novelist. Dan McCall's memoir of his golden-boy youth in the 1950s, when he won national speech contests with patriotic paeans to America's dream of itself, appeared on the *Today* program, and took part in a rigged TV game show, is a compelling portrayal of that time and this country—and an entertaining if awful depiction of the price paid for being a child prodigy."

— Ed Zuckerman
Executive Producer and Writer, *Law and Order*

Praise for
Boy on a Unicycle:
Confessions of a Young Man Trained to be a Winner

"Dan McCall has written beautifully about the problems of being at the top, the national champion of this or that. To be there is to be left with all the devices and forces of competition that got you there idled in your new eminence. No resistance anywhere, no one else to defeat; one's polished dynamics not able to function at large. Oneself the object of one's contrivances."

— A. R. Ammons
winner of the National Book Award for Poetry

"From beginning to end the author takes a distinct pleasure in evoking these days of his youth, and the reader just as great a pleasure in reading about them. For twenty-plus years Dan McCall was the nation's boy, and in every sense he lived up to the role."

— Lamar Herrin
author of *The Lies Boys Tell* and *Fractures*

"Dan McCall's prose moves with clarity and assurance, having nothing to prove, and so much to offer."

— Wayne Gladstone
author of *Notes From the Internet Apocalypse*

"Dan McCall engages and enchants the reader by creating vivid images with a few select words…. A thrilling discovery from a classic American writer, told with heart, honesty, and style."

— Kirsten Lobe
author of *Paris Hangover*

Also by
Dan McCall

Citizens of Somewhere Else
Messenger Bird
Triphammer
The Silence of Bartleby
Queen of Hearts
Bluebird Canyon
Beecher
Jack the Bear
The Man Says Yes
The Example of Richard Wright

BOY ON A UNICYCLE

confessions of a
young man trained
to be a winner

For Evan

CONTENTS

Foreword	i
ONE: BEFORE AND AFTER *PART ONE: A CHRISTMAS REVENGE* *PART TWO: COLLAPSE*	1
TWO: OPTIMISM FOR COURAGEOUS LIVING	9
THREE: BOY ON A UNICYCLE	30
FOUR: THE MODESTO KID	44
FIVE: THE CONFESSIONS OF JOHNNY APPLESEED	67
SIX: CYRANO	81
SEVEN: PROUD PATRIOTS AND ENLIGHTENED CITIZENS	97
EIGHT: STRIKE IT RICH	113
NINE: A STANFORD MAN *PART ONE: THE BARGAIN* *PART TWO: I'M GOING TO BE A WRITER*	128
TEN: HOME AGAIN	157
ELEVEN: THE FAR SIDE OF THE WORLD *PART ONE: IT'S ALL DOWNHILL FROM HERE* *PART TWO: CALCUTTA*	177
TWELVE: L'ENVOI	193
Afterword	209
Acknowledgments	214

FOREWORD

"Dan McCall is a writer, God help him!"
— *Tennessee Williams*

For Dan McCall, writing was both a calling and an obsession. I hold on to the image of my Dad at his desk, scotch in hand, banging away at his Royal manual typewriter through a haze of cigarette smoke. After his death in 2012, following a career as a Professor of American Literature at Cornell University, I found myself sorting through mountains of pages in his home in Ithaca, NY. Among manuscripts in various stages of completion, I soon focused on the one project he was most passionate about: his memoir.

For more than forty years Dan would write his story and then abandon it, only to take up the project again a decade later. He was never able to settle on a final version, and it was never published.

Boy on a Unicycle tells of a 1950s teen prodigy with a particular gift for enthralling audiences with speeches about American optimism. By his senior year of high school, Dan McCall had won an unprecedented three National Championships in Oratory. Was this the best thing that ever happened to him, or the worst? This memoir, a mixture of pride and shame, was written by a man who never could answer that question.

Dan McCall's memoir is, in part, a contemplation of America's continuing nostalgia for the 1950s. My father's autobiographical quest is an echo of one of his heroes, James Agee, who writes: "Is the world out there in the present always some talisman of the world inside me, in my past? ... Do I dare to hope that my own story could become an emblem, some statement in the idiom of personality for a cultural experience?"

This memoir represents my father's bravest attempt to explore the depths of his soul. I am honored, at long last, to share his story.

— Steven McCall

CHAPTER ONE

BEFORE AND AFTER

PART ONE
A Christmas Revenge

"The first and deepest of all my wishes is to give satisfaction to my parents."
— John Quincy Adams

"Every child forms his first image of what is 'bad', quite concretely, by what is forbidden—by his parents' prohibitions, taboos, and fears."
— Alice Miller, *The Drama of the Gifted Child*

"POISE: Attended Dr. and Mrs. Harris' Tea for Mrs. Frost, November 14, 1941. Danny Boy said 'How-do' and shook hands with all guests. Sat quietly on small stool, crossed legs, took only one cookie when they were passed, said 'Sank you' and in general was restrained and yet completely at ease."
— Velma McCall, "Comments on Mental Habits Which Should Be Acquired," *Our Baby*

Christmas Day 1946, Eugene, Oregon

We were where we belonged, the House on the Hill. I stood tall to be measured in the pantry, my name and height were marked there below the marks of my twin cousins, and now in the twilight Robert and Richard were throwing around a new football in the great expanse of emerald yard. I stayed inside to entertain the adults. I could spread my legs and bend over very slowly and touch my head to the vast Oriental rug and —without putting my hands down—straighten up to stand tall again. A brave little soldier, I saluted.

Uncle Frank and Aunt Peggy and the boys went home in their Christmas present from Gram and Gramps, a green Cadillac. I played with Chinese Checker marbles on that big Oriental rug.

Suddenly it was too quiet. I looked up.

Mom and Daddy and Gram and Gramps, all four of them, were staring at me. They slowly ushered me into the candlelit dining room, to the immense table with the twelve upholstered chairs.

Something was up, something big.

I looked from face to face. Another gift? Gosh, I'd already had so many. But was there one more?

They just stood there. And then Gramps pulled out a crisp heavy paper with writing on it. Slowly in his rich voice he explained to me that it was a "bargain." As he talked, his daughter, Mom, came to me and gently tried to put me at ease. Daddy was oddly silent and still, standing a little apart, at the mahogany buffet.

I stared at the parchment on the dark gleaming table. Here, Gramps said, was the deal: if I would promise not to drink liquor until I was twenty-one years of age, if I would faithfully keep my written pledge, then I would be rewarded on my twenty-first birthday with a cash prize of $1,000.

Mom, standing behind me, her hands on my shoulders, repeated in a whisper, "A *thousand dollars.*"

Then, silence. Like praying in church.

I knew how to print my name. Dan E. McCall. E. for Elliott, Gram's maiden name. My parents picked it out because if you say Dan E. real fast it sounds like Danny.

The dining room was all dark and flickery in the candlelight. I looked at the fountain pen. I looked at the bargain. Mom moved back and stood with Daddy at the buffet. Gram said Robert and Richard had done it, the twins had signed the very same pledge when they were my age.

I wanted desperately to please—I could tell this was a test, to see what I was made of. But it was all too big. I couldn't seem to hold the pen right, it got mixed up, the pen scratched and stalled. So Gramps did it with me, guiding my hand as I formed the letters, DAN E. McCALL. My grandfather's ruby ring. My little boy hand in his big man's hand.

Afterwards, back in the rich freedom of the ornate living room, I bent over and put my head down on the Oriental carpet, stood up, and saluted. Everybody clapped just as before. But I felt funny. My head didn't hurt and I didn't have a stomach ache. Still, I wasn't myself. I said I had something very important to tell them. I made them be quiet. Then I solemnly announced I was afraid that I had swallowed one of the Chinese Checker marbles.

I don't know why I told them that. I was all confused. Funny things were going on. First, Mom was "pregnant." Inside her huge round tummy was my little brother—or sister—waiting to come out and play with me. Daddy spent all day in Gramps' study reading over all those long sheets of paper. Mom said he was 'correcting galleys' of his big book about how to give a speech. Both my parents were neglecting me. And now I wasn't allowed to use the toilet. I had to poop in a bucket. Poor Daddy said he'd have to sift through it with a stick. On the morning of the third day, still no marble.

When I'd made up the story I hadn't realized it would mean all this trouble. But I couldn't say, now, that I had *lied*. So I strolled silently into Gram and Gramps' empty living room. I looked around. After a while I wandered over to the teak table, opened the Chinese Checker box, and extracted a blue marble. I carried it in my left pants pocket all the rest of the afternoon. During candlelight dinner I could feel the marble hard and little and round against my leg.

That night, astride my silver bucket, after I'd finished my business but before I called Daddy, I stood up and pulled the marble out of my pocket. I turned around and dropped it, bombs-away, into the bucket.

Daddy came back and I waited, carefully.

My father crouched, picked up his stick, then leaned forward and muttered, "There."

I exploded with gladness, suddenly innocent. Hardly taking time to button up, I raced out to tell Mom and Gram and Gramps about my success.

And when I was finally tucked in for the night, in my little cot at the foot of my parents' bed, I was perfectly happy. Mom came in, at last, and softly sang me my own lullaby, in her high, beautiful voice:

> Oh Danny boy, the pipes, the pipes are calling
> From glen to glen, and down the mountain side.
> Oh Danny boy, oh Danny boy, I love you so.

Falling asleep I laughed out loud into my pillow. What a Christmas! I wasn't just a kid anymore. Now I was a real member of the family.

PART TWO
Collapse

"All confession, literary or sacramental, is either a lie or the record of a conversion, a death and a resurrection. Self-knowledge is necessarily death of the self, a descent into Hell, while self-expression in its profoundest sense is necessarily re-birth."
— John Freccero

Summer 1961, Calcutta, India

I never should have come to Calcutta alone.

Under the brown blanket of baggy monsoon clouds, heat was indistinguishable from steaming wet skin and starving mud. Beggars slept on the sidewalk; at night they dropped their purple bodies on the mats and in damp, shredded cots along the gutters. Everyone was dying around me, every man, woman, and child in the endless urban swamp. The world is a waste, a terrible hurting waste, and it's not fair for all of this to happen—

In my hotel room I pulled out six finger bowls, delicate silver, gifts for Mom and Dad and Dave (*what the fuck does my kid brother want with finger bowls?*), and got out my bottle of Johnnie Walker to drink a toast from each one—

I couldn't tell whether it was the Scotch or a severe reaction to all those shots, I'd had cholera shots and typhus shots and yellow fever shots, Jesus, I thought I was gonna black out—

Drink up!

I sat naked at my desk and pulled out a piece of stationery, staring at my cramped fingers scrawling O's, a penmanship exercise. I signed my name, pretending Gramps was there, guiding my hand. Ladies and gentlemen: there's your perfect bargain.

Oh grandfather I broke my promise to you—

But you had no right to extract that promise from me—

So maybe I could blame it all on you, grandfather, I could say, 'Yep, he turned the glory of the grape into

Forbidden Fruit—that's the fashion, so blame it on Gramps, or on Mother and Dad, all my pain is their fault, but that would be so—so—cowardly.

If I were to write a book about my life, Mother and Dad would be alarmed, would be dismayed, would be hurt beyond words, and why, for *what*? How could I ever do that to my beloved parents, who did things for me that I'll never understand, although I know that in their steady devotion they gave all they had to me—where and how does one start to rearrange and de-arrange the needs of loved ones without being ungrateful?

More Scotch!

It's serious, Dan, that El Stinko killing you is the horrible disease that your gorgeous grandfather was trying to warn you against in the way that made sense for him—all sorts of good grampas set goals for their grandsons—he just meant a gold watch or something—and at least he was a MAN, at least he knew that a man *pays* for whatever integrity he rescues from this life, whatever honor and truth he painfully pulls out of the slop, and you better love him for that, revere him for that, be fair for once in your fake life—and it is a fake, sucker, you have ground yourself down all over the planet to the fact that this bleeding mess you have on your hands is exactly what you were, and you weren't an American boy, you weren't an All-American boy, you were a Professional American boy—

And now, in the Black Hole of Calcutta, I'm having a catastrophic collapse.

CHAPTER TWO

OPTIMISM FOR COURAGEOUS LIVING

"The person who is 'grandiose' is admired everywhere, and needs this admiration; indeed, he cannot live without it. He must excel brilliantly in everything he undertakes, which he is surely capable of doing (otherwise he just does not attempt it). He, too, admires himself, for his qualities—his beauty, cleverness, talents—and for his success and achievements. Beware if one of these fails him—love is not forthcoming without achievement. We have to despise everything in ourselves that is not wonderful, good, and clever. This means further: 'Without these achievements, these gifts, I could never be loved, would never have been loved.'"
— Alice Miller, *The Drama of the Gifted Child*

"But to what extent did I believe in my delirium? That's the basic question, and yet I can't tell. I lived beyond my years as one lives beyond one's means: with zeal, with fatigue, at great cost, for the sake of display. How can one put on an act without knowing that one is acting?"
 — Jean-Paul Sartre, *The Words*

"America loves a winner."
 — General George Patton

1952, Eugene, Oregon

My life in speech contests began in April of 1952, when Mother registered me for the Optimist International oratory competition. Dad had just finished his book, *Fundamentals of Speech*, and Mother thought I'd be a natural. The very first round at Roosevelt Junior High in Eugene had only four of us participants—I was in seventh grade and the other three in ninth. I'd never been in a speech contest before, and hardly knew what to expect. We all practiced together after school in the cafeteria.

The day of that first round I ascended to the cafeteria rostrum. It was very strange. My voice surprised me, it was naked, and it bounced over their heads and back from the pale green walls. I was looking at the walls, losing the eye-contact I had practiced in the mirror. I was speaker number three, my only real competition had just finished, and now I was going to show them the magic. But my voice, my voice:

> "In 1944 at the time of the battle of Attu there occurred a dramatic story of gallantry and tragedy. Six navy fliers, whose plane had crashed in a raging sea, were clinging desperately to rubber life-rafts in zero weather. Above them circled a plane, sending out radio messages for rescue ships. But darkness was falling, and no ships had come.
>
> Finally, the pilot of the plane decided to take a thousand-to-one chance of coming

down in the rampaging sea to rescue them. But the men on the rafts, seeing the hazard to both man and plane, waved, —*and here, my first gesture, both hands held up, shoulder high, palms out*—'Don't land!' *Hands slowly, not mechanically, back to my sides.* The pilot of the plane accepted their decision and flew away. Three days later, after the storm was over, planes re-discovered the rafts. All six men on them were dead."

My face was itching, everywhere, a fly crawling around on it. My eyes watered. In the audience Mother's face was reassuring, she was calm now; the frown she'd given me from before was gone. Earlier, when I was sitting in my chair up there on the stage, waiting my turn, and patting my hair into place, Mother's frown told me that I shouldn't be doing that while another contestant was speaking.

"This incident of heroism was only one of many during the Great War in which American boys lived and died courageously, because—they were optimists. They were not fair-weather optimists, who fit the definition of optimism as a disposition to be hopeful, or cheerful, but more religious and profound optimists, who believed that the order of things in the universe is adapted to produce the greatest good."

Nearing the end, the timer in the front row bent over his stop watch and motioned that I had passed the four minute mark—if you came in under four or went over five, you lost points. I finished up at 4:33, ten seconds under my usual practice time.

Later there would be punch and cookies. About thirty people in the junior high cafeteria, teachers and parents and Optimists. The social studies teacher who had coached us for a month was sitting in the front row, arms folded, in a gray suit.

I figured that Wally, the Student Body President, was my real competition; he was so *confident*. His girl, a cheerleader, sat all dressed up in blue at the exact middle of the room. The third guy was a weird-o (he read comic books in English class and giggled all the time). The fourth boy, Keith, was extremely tall, the starting center on the Roughriders basketball team. He had a strange speech: he actually came to Optimism after the death of his pet dog. [Not me, I'd already had a dog who died on me—Christopher, named after Christopher Columbus, since he was always exploring. Christopher was given to me when I was six, a beautiful Fox Terrier puppy—I'll never forget when Dad and I brought him home, and Mom came down from upstairs and crouched on the landing with her arms open wide. God, I loved to play with him on the kitchen floor while the folks were doing the dishes. But one day, right in front of my eyes, Christopher ran into the street and got run over by a beer truck. He was my best friend. Dead. Then and there I made a vow: No More Pets. All they do is break your heart.] But here in the Optimist Club's speech contest, Keith had lost his dog, and the death, well, somehow it gave him… Optimism! No wonder he didn't stand a chance.

We had to eat the cookies and drink the punch

and be polite with everybody and listen to all that "I wouldn't want to be a judge ha ha you're all winners" while the three Toastmasters huddled in the back with their ballots. Mother was shining, radiant, and she gave me a wink that said there was no question, and she talked graciously with the other boys.

When the decision was reached we had to go back on the stage. It was pretty terrible, though, because the judges only announced first place (Me), second place (Wally the Student Body President), and third place (the giggle boy)—and Keith the Canine Optimist sitting next to me on the stage let out a groan. It was an awful little moan, all the way up from his huge shoes, and I suddenly stared at him and then away very fast; I had worried all along about beating Wally, but the moan made it clear that Keith never saw anything above third and was counting on it. He didn't think he would win, but he couldn't bear being *last*.

When we got home Mom and I played a little trick on Dad. He hadn't been able to come because he had to speak somewhere and so we told him Wally had won, it was really a bum decision, and Dad was very disappointed because he was, after all, the Chairman of the Speech Department at the University of Oregon and we had worked together on that speech. But then while Dad sat at the kitchen table, dejection, I went down to the basement and got my suitcase. "Oh, all right, I'll go to Boise." That would be in a month, the section finals, four western states and three Canadian provinces.

He jumped up, all right again, looking from mother to me.

We worked together, father and son, every day for the

next four weeks on that speech, on the right inflection for every word, the proper speed for every sentence. That first paragraph about the Navy fliers was such a powerful story on its own, the job wasn't to ham it up. You let tragedy speak for itself. Don't get excited. Be calm. Be clear. Gestures are crucial, you have to know what to do with your hands. At the beginning, practicing the signal for "Don't Land," I got the idea but had trouble doing it, so Dad and I stood facing each other, working it out together. With the simple, grave motion of my hands, I was his mirror image. In May Mother and I took the train to Boise for the sectional finals. All the contestants seemed so much bigger and older than I. The rumor around Convention Center was that the real competition, a boy named Gerry Tester from Vancouver, would take it hands-down, just as he had the previous year. He wasn't even arriving until dinner time just before the competition on Saturday.

I worried that maybe I was cheating because Dad wrote every word of my speech. This was supposed to be "*Original* Oratory." My science teacher at Roosevelt Junior High smelled a rat; he surprised me during a biology quiz. Leaning down at my desk he asked an extra question just for me: spell and define "Thermopylae." He seemed taken aback when I knew about the unsuccessful Spartan stand. Dad had written all the words, of course, but he explained every one of them to me. And in Boise one kid said that when he gave his speech he used notes—I didn't know you could do that —and another kid bragged that his "original" oration was written by a professional journalist. As I listened to the other guys, all of whom were bigger and stronger than me, I *knew* they hadn't written those words. So

I was off the hook. But still, every single word—and how to say every single word—was Dad's. He was a ventriloquist and I was his dummy.

The other boys didn't think much of me, but liked me well enough because I was so small and probably no competition. I finally caught sight of Gerry Tester in the hotel: he was very tall and lean and blond, in a glossy suit, and his voice was richly modulated, oratorical, just talking with the Optimists who remembered him from the year before. Besides me, he was the only contestant whose mother came along.

It was a fairly long, narrow stuffy auditorium, packed. People were sitting in windows, all around the floor, and standing in back. We drew for speaking positions and again I was number three:

> This characteristic is what I would call the 'priceless ingredient' of life. The idea comes from the story of the wise man of Ancient Baghdad, who was called upon one day by a young man of the town who asked, "How shall I buy wisely?"
>
> "In all things," replied the wise man, "look for that which can neither be bought nor sold —the priceless ingredient."
>
> "The 'priceless ingredient?'" said the young man. "How shall I look for it? How shall I recognize it?"
>
> *Right arm up, half-extended, not jerky but with conviction, the fist closed, but not too tight, and the index finger pointing:*
>
> "The 'priceless ingredient,' said the wiseman, "is the integrity of the maker."

> *Pause. Quietly, with the index finger extended, the truth:* "Look for the integrity of the maker."

There was no applause allowed, but when I finished and walked on out to the contestants' room there was considerable murmuring. My spirit sank after Gerry Tester finished: a sharp burst of real, spontaneous applause. The Head Judge warned the audience.

The big kid from Portland was satisfied with third place. Gerry Tester, smiling bravely, was sick with second. The trophy was small but heavy, gold, a man standing with his arm on a tablet where a jeweler could engrave my name. That night in the hotel eight of us played penny-ante poker. Gerry laughed, "Hey, this guy wins everything." Afterwards I went back up to the room where Mother was waiting, my pockets and hands full of pennies. Mom told me I had to take the money back. I returned to the door of the poker room, but I couldn't go in and give the guys their pennies back, I just couldn't. So I took another elevator trip, went into the big speech contest room, it was all dark, I couldn't find the lights, and I piled all the pennies on the dais. On the train trip home I polished my trophy with Kleenexes, polished it for miles and miles.

While waiting for the National Finals in Louisville in June, a record was mailed to me from national headquarters, a recording of the previous year's Optimist Oratory Winner. Listening to it, I got my own speech all fouled up. The 1951 winner was a practitioner of old time declamation, fire and brimstone; the most thrilling part of his speech was when he quoted the Dean of some Law School addressing an ill-prepared class in

1942: *"Gentlemen, if you let a little thing like a war stop you, you will never become lawyers!!"* Those roars and elaborate inflections began to creep into my delivery. I even memorized his first minute ("A century ago, the English statesman Benjamin Disraeli said, 'The burden of tomorrow's problems falls upon the youth of today…'") and I tried to imitate his voice exactly. I boomed "Don't Land!" in my opening illustration. Mother and Dad kept coming into the study to tell me to stop. I protested that he had *won*, talking that way. They said that *he* had won, talking that way, but *I* wouldn't. Mom even cried about it—she said I wasn't "natural" anymore. And Dad disapproved; he was a leading advocate of the "conversational style." So, before I went to Louisville, they convinced me to go back to my old way. Besides, I couldn't get near that booming voice—and I could kind of tell that you shouldn't be so forceful until your voice changed. But it bothered me to hear myself on tape, I sounded so young.

When Mother and I finally got off the plane in Louisville, the temperature and the humidity were both in the nineties, my brown tweed pants were damply digging into my legs, my ears wouldn't pop and my throat was on fire. Our room in the Henry Clay wasn't air-conditioned. Mother had room service send up ice cubes, and she put them in a little white towel and held it to my head. My fever was 101; I'd been perfectly okay in Eugene that morning, so maybe I'd picked up a bug in Chicago. And then, after dinner, I got frightened by some drunk Optimists. They came laughing out of the bar, didn't see me standing there sick, and almost knocked me down. The inebriated Conventioneers seemed like an omen—I might not even make it past the semi-finals.

At three a.m. I awoke and tried to practice my speech in the bathroom, but my voice was nasal and I threw up during my second illustration. I was drenched with sweat and my legs were rubbery. The only thing that seemed to help was for me to sit in a hot tub, hot as I could stand it. I got a little more practice on my speech, sitting in the steam, ice cubes melting on my forehead. I dried off, got into my pajamas, and a Negro bellhop brought us tea and toast at 6:30; Mother was in the bathroom, and I had to tip him. I gave him a dime. He looked at it, and he looked at me. He said, "Whatever you prefer." Then he slammed the shit out of the door.

My temperature climbed a degree to a hundred and two. The doctor saw us at 8:30. He was from the North, and talked like us; he gave me a shot of penicillin and swabbed my throat. I still hadn't met any of the competition, although I had seen several tall good-looking boys walking around the lobby. I had to stay in bed all day, and missed the round-up of boys for the tours of Churchill Downs and the Louisville Slugger plant. The doctor from the North stopped by that evening and stabbed me full of more penicillin. He talked in the hall with Mother. For dinner she had them bring me a steak-burger and green salad and lemonade. I read movie magazines until midnight and slept through until seven.

My white suit was ready when I awoke: white linen, double-breasted, bone buttons, we had had our tailor make it up special in Eugene, my costume for the National Finals: a perfect little gentleman, white threads in the blue grass. I got it on, with exquisite care, Mom timed my speech, 4:43, right on the button, and we went down for breakfast. At last a familiar face: the 13th District Commander, a lean sun-burned redhead from Montana, stopped at our table: "We know you'll do us proud, Danny." He'd seen my triumph in Boise.

The Finalists had to sit for a group picture: twenty-seven of us, and some of them were enormous and a few actually smoked. Three of them had been in the previous year's Championship, and they were smooth, polished, laughing together. There was only one boy as short as I was—he was wearing a red jacket and blue slacks and white shirt and bow tie with white stars on a blue field. Dope. But I was way out of my league, my voice sounded puny next to the big guys' basso profondos. Tears came to my eyes as I sat smiling for that group picture. Poor little creature, I had no chance at all. It was so obviously unfair. Their big sonorous voices, my little boy's voice. They were all Goliath—and I was—it suddenly struck me—David. I'm little and all alone, and that's why you can't beat me. I *am* Optimism. I *am* this country, 13 little colonies that beat the bejeezus out of The British Empire!

Fourteen of us competed in the main ballroom, which wasn't air-conditioned; the other semi-finals got the dining room at 72 degrees. I drew lucky Speaker #3 —the same position I'd had in Eugene and Boise:

> "In *Time* Magazine in 1944, at the time of the battle of Attu, there appeared a dramatic story of gallantry and tragedy. Six Navy fliers…"

From that opening paragraph on I did it all perfectly, just the way Dad and I had practiced it a thousand times. Dad had taught me how to say all of the words exactly right. But when I finished and walked off the stage, I didn't feel lucky as I sat there listening to that long parade of tall guys following me. The Ohio boy's big moment was the vision at the end of his speech: "I see a man, walking by the shore of a Galilean Lake," and it was very effective. I was angry that Dad and I had neglected to put Jesus in my speech. By the time we had all finished, the afternoon sun was pouring into the room, and people were fanning themselves with programs. Three speakers from each section would be chosen for the Final Round.

When Mom and I called home to Dad that night, I told him that someone had seen the ballots and the rumor was I had the highest score of the three from my section. Dad warned me, "Be careful, son—don't let your hopes get too high."

Some of the losers went home, but most of them stayed, and everybody took a long damp tour of Mammoth Cave and My Old Kentucky Home. It was swell, but I was worried about the boy from Glendale, California—he hadn't been in my semi-finals—the reports said his closing illustration from Abraham Lincoln was championship stuff.

All the contestants were invited to a country club for a swim. Mother told me I shouldn't go in the water, because of my cold, and I promised her I wouldn't. The Glendale boy was doing some jackknives off the high board. Mr. Unbeatable. I rented swim trunks in the locker room and climbed the ladder while Glendale stood dripping beside the board. OK. I did a swan with a half-twist so perfectly that I laughed out loud under the water. I hopped out. Now it was my turn to stand dripping beside the board. I looked at Glendale, and he looked at me. We both knew what life was all about.

That night in our room, Mom was panicky: my temperature was 103.

The Finals were at two o'clock. The Crystal Ballroom was packed with over a thousand Optimists and Opti-Mrs. All around the walls hung flags of local clubs, with a huge poster at the front: "OPTIMISM: THE FAITH THAT LEADS TO ACHIEVEMENT." Mother sat in her lucky green dress, halfway back, under one of the enormous glass chandeliers. There was a podium with a microphone for the men who had conducted the meeting, but the mike was unplugged and the podium was carted away for the finals of the Boys' Oratorical Contest.

It was all on the line now. My fever relaxed me. On my way to the stage in my freshly pressed white suit, I exchanged greetings with the doctor from the North —he wasn't an Optimist, of course, he had come to the finals just because I was his patient; he had an umbrella between his legs. It was raining outside, cooling things off at last. In the course of my speech I made my deepest eye-contact with three people: Mom in the middle of a sea of faces, the Northern doctor down front, and way in the back a badly sunburned man with a white crewcut. In conclusion:

> "When Harry Emerson Fosdick was a young man in college, he wrote a letter to his future wife telling her that although he had

not yet met her, and did not know who she was, he knew that somewhere she was alive and waiting for him. And in that letter he promised to keep his fidelity to her as true as though she were already his."

There are a half-dozen different ways of saying those two sentences, and Dad and I had tried them all, in his study in Eugene. I liked this part the best: it was like a game-winning basket or a touchdown pass, going through my mind in slow motion. Mother and Dad had bought me a unicycle for my birthday, and I'd learned how to pause and sit rocking in place; now, when I got to Fosdick's letter to his future wife, I felt somehow mounted, perfect, and the audience could sense it, too. A hush came over them. It broke my heart when I said "as true as though she were already his."

I had to say those words as if it weren't practiced and rehearsed. I had to do it as if it were all happening naturally. Dad said the job was "to make the audience a family." His hazel eyes told me: the way you do it is to go under the words. The words are only a way to get there. When you're really cooking, when you've got it, the words aren't words anymore. My father said to me, "All words aspire to silence." Funny thing to say, for a man who teaches you how to talk.

In that final round, that afternoon in Louisville, I did it better than I had in Eugene. Better than in Boise. I was Dan E. McCall, twelve years old, joining my life to a thousand adults in the Crystal Ballroom.

The official rulebook granted maximum points in two categories:

> 30 points for subject matter (includes originality, coherence and logic)
> 70 points for delivery and poise (the power to thrill and impress)

The boy from Glendale sure did thrill and impress. He took a little walk about half-way through his speech, a couple of steps, steps of conviction. I hadn't walked at all, I had been rooted to the spot. Listening, watching, I couldn't tell whether his walk would pay off. I should have walked. Next time I'll walk. In the middle you take three or four steps, and then turn, one hand casually moving back to the area you have covered. Good move.

There was an intermission. Down front, the judges got together and sat huddled with their ballots. I couldn't get to Mother through the crowd. I threaded my way out to a drinking fountain on the mezzanine. The boy from Iowa who had lost in the semi-finals grabbed me, smiling, and showed me his unofficial score card: "I have you picked for second," he said, as if that would encourage me.

Second? Are you kidding? Runner-up? And those Navy pilots—those men on the rubber rafts in zero weather—is self-sacrifice an also-ran?

I strolled around on the thick green carpet. If people thought I had won, they smiled at me; if they thought I hadn't, they looked away. I pretended to be lost in thought. I was the boy in the white suit.

Finally, the announcement was made by a bald man from Los Angeles, the Retiring President who had warned the general session about "the subversive elements desperately eager to capture the mind and hearts of our young people." The kid from Utica, New

York got third. I hadn't expected that; he wore thick rimless glasses, a kind of bookish boy. But that was okay, come to think of it, that was a good third. I sat there, staring at my hands, my fingers, the delicate blue veins of my wrist. Was I going to win this thing or not? Mom and Dad had worked so hard, and I had too. Oh, this was too much for me, it hurt—I was being changed—I couldn't take it—I couldn't. I prayed, Oh God, dearest Father, please give me this, and I'll never bother you again.

It was June 28, 1952. My father's 46th birthday.

The bald man toyed, or seemed to toy, with the scorecards in his hand. "Let's see here, our second place winner, the runner-up today is…" He peered at the cards, pretending to be confused, "The winner of second place is…"

I sat there promising God everything I owed him, everything I ever would, a whole lifetime of service.

"Yes, from my own home state of California…"

Glendale was *second*! I burst forward, my eyes swimming up to the crystal chandeliers and going crazy in their brilliant white radiance. I didn't need God the Father anymore, I had my own father, Dad. Outside it had stopped raining. The air suddenly felt fresh. I glanced at the Texas boy, the lip-nibbling dude who after all still thought maybe he could be the champion. People around me weren't crushing me or slapping me on the shoulder yet. They didn't know. They should have. I certainly did.

Then, in a huge hush: "Our National Champion for 1952—Dan E. McCall."

Applause!, wonderful, gorgeous applause—big billowy waves of it—a thousand people deeply, rhythmically clapping and whistling and lifting. The doctor from the North was standing up holding aloft his umbrella and tapping the air. A man was leading Mother up to the stage, Mother in her lucky green dress.

Next morning our mailbox at the Henry Clay reception desk was stuffed with a dozen telegrams. People in Eugene said they were "bursting with pride." Then Mom and I were on our way home. At the layover in Chicago we ate turkey sandwiches in the Sky Room, and she said with a mischievous wink, "You're not a boy anymore—you're a National Champion." I didn't know what to say. I'd never been a boy, actually.

In the gift shop I scanned the paperback books. Back in Eugene, Willy Black, throwing rocks at his Dalmatian puppy, had told me about *I, the Jury*. Now, in O'Hare airport, while Mom was occupied, I bought the dirty book. In our plane winging westward I read some of the juicy parts, especially that last page. Wow. I took off my shoes and stretched out. I still had a little fever; totally exhausted, I fell asleep. But in my sleep, gradually, I felt something fantastic, something completely new and crazy and frightening, the seat-belt across my lap rubbing against me, everything getting all hot and weird, painful and joyful, both at the same time, and then—*then*—I bolted awake. At first I didn't know what had happened or where I was. I looked down at Mom's hand, on my hand, on the arm-rest. The flashy jeweled ring on her finger. Mom was sleeping, or pretending to sleep.

Very quietly I sat up. I tip-toed in my stocking feet down the aisle into the lavatory. In there I inspected, and wiped the sticky stuff off my belly with toilet paper.

In my socks I came back down the aisle and lowered myself back into the seat beside Mom who was still sleeping, I guess—I guess she was sleeping. I sat there— Was this what a National Champion feels like? Was what just happened the real prize? My face felt different. My shoulders felt different. I was another person.

Jesus, was Mom really asleep?

At the Eugene airport a gray sky was full of rain, but when Mother and I stepped off the plane, cheers went up. A big line of cars had "DANNY" and "WINNER" and "CHAMP" poster-paint signs on the doors. Some Roosevelt kids were there, and we had a parade down Willamette, cops on motorcycles with their sirens going, and a reception in the Roosevelt cafeteria. Dad had a camera, making a home movie of it. But Dad hardly looked me in the eye, almost as if he were embarrassed. He couldn't seem to get into the spirit of the occasion. Wasn't this Roy C. McCall's triumph? Ever since I'd got off the plane I had been waiting for him to hug me or kiss me. But he didn't.

All the girls made a big fuss over David. Marjorie Caulkins came up and hugged me and told me my little brother was "a living doll." And he was. He was sweet, he was instinctively nice, not like me. You could see it in his clear, beautiful eyes. Pissed me off.

The next day, in the newspaper:

Eugene Register-Guard
Sunday, June 29, 1952, front page:

A kid with a sore throat Saturday won the Optimist International oratorical finals at the service organization's national competition in Louisville, KY. It was his first venture of that kind, but 12-year-old Danny McCall came away with a $1,000 college scholarship. Son of the chairman of the University of Oregon speech department, Danny bested a big field of contestants, ranging up to 17 years old, with his five-minute oration on 'Optimism for Courageous Living.'

After word of Danny's victory reached Eugene, his dad—Dr. Roy C. McCall— reported that he had talked with his wife and son in Louisville, and learned (1): That Danny almost missed the finals because of a throat infection; (2) Danny asked on the phone, "Isn't God good to me?"; and (3) Danny and his mother will arrive at Eugene's Mahlon Sweet Airport Tuesday morning.

The first thing Danny will want to do, his Dad opined, will be to go swimming.

On their return to Eugene Danny is to be met by a big parade arranged by the Optimists and Danny is to be installed as the nation's champion in big ceremonies.

The following year I was nominated for President of the Roosevelt Junior High School Student Body. I made my campaign posters myself with colored pencils. The other candidate, Bobby Overstreet, had poster parties, a dozen kids painting together, using bright rich paints on huge posters that they put up on the pale green walls above the lockers. But I did mine all by myself in my room, busy as a bee, listening to the radio.

At school I put up my posters:

>D ependable
>A greeable
>N ational C hampion

After I lost, I talked it over with Walter Osborn, shooting hoops in the rain in my driveway. Walter said I shouldn't have put "National Champion" on my posters. A lot of the kids had thought that was braggy.

It clicked in my head—oh, of course—other people can call you a National Champion, but you yourself can't say that's who you are. How could I have been so dumb?

Walter had been on the committee that counted the ballots, and he said I lost by a mile. It wasn't even close. Bobby Overstreet won in a landslide. I couldn't figure out why Walter had to emphasize how badly I'd gotten beat. Then he smiled kind of sadly and said he had to go home, he wasn't supposed to "play" with me. Walter said, with a sick grin on his face, "My Dad says you're 'a precocious little shit.'"

That hurt. Sure, I knew I was precocious—but I also knew I was a little shit.

Alone, I shot lay-ups and played 'Horse' against myself in the rain. I rode my unicycle, a present for my birthday, up and down the alley. Bobby Overstreet gave a dumb speech. God, it was dumb. But the kids liked it. Kids don't care what you *say*.

I pedaled out into the street in the rain.

I pedaled over to the U. of O. I didn't want to be who I was. I mean, who people thought Dan E. McCall was. On the little bike-path through the cemetery opposite McArthur Court I was getting drenched, but I liked it. I thought of the umbrella the Northern doctor in Louisville had held up when I won. I made my way on the winding path among the tombstones. What was *wrong* with me? The kids laughed at my campaign speech. Damn it! The kids laughed at my salutation: "Fellow students—" Mom said they were just jealous. Mom always said that. It wasn't true. But who cared, anyway? Mom and Dad truly loved me. I wondered, though, would they love me if I hadn't won? Would my parents still have loved me if Dan E. McCall was a loser? Did anybody love you just for who you were, when you weren't performing? I wanted to be loved because I was nobody. Absolutely nobody.

I pedaled out into the wet gravel roadway. A blonde college girl was walking along in a hurry, probably taking a short-cut to class. I got so lost in her that I failed to mind my own business. The uni got away from me and I fell off backwards down onto the muddy gravel. The girl turned, stared at me, and suddenly burst out laughing.

I sat there in the mud. In the graveyard. Then I picked myself up and went over beside the huge oak tree to steady myself while I got back up on my unicycle. That beautiful girl was laughing at me. Well, everybody was. Everybody. I wasn't a National Champion, I was a Precocious Little Shit.

I looked at my muddy hand on the soaking tree, my fingers digging into the wet bark. The whole world was silent, except for the deliberate sound of the heavy raindrops on the big leaves of the somber trees. I mounted up. And Dan E. McCall slowly rode his unicycle back into the audience of wet tombstones.

CHAPTER THREE

BOY ON A UNICYCLE

"In early youth, as we contemplate our coming life, we are like children in a theater before the curtain is raised, sitting there in high spirits and eagerly waiting for the play to begin. It is a blessing that we do not know what is really going to happen. We are like lambs in the field, disporting themselves under the eyes of the butcher."
— Arthur Schopenhauer

"False empowerment lifts the child up to an inordinately powerful position, pumping up, or at least not appropriately checking, the child's grandiosity. A disorder of self-esteem. We raise boys to live in a world in which they are either winners or losers."
— Terrence Real,
I Don't Want To Talk About It

"I don't want to go around pretending to be me."
— Philip Larkin

1953-1954, Roosevelt Junior High, Eugene, Oregon

The unicycle was the best birthday present I ever got. It was a total surprise; Mom and Dad had it built especially for me by a guy at a bicycle store. I learned how to ride it in our driveway. It was really hard. Mom laughed; she said it looked impossible. But within a week I was pedaling it all over the neighborhood. A man in a pickup truck stopped, grinned, got out and tried it, and busted his ass. His wife called to him from the truck, told him to stop making a damn fool of himself.

I decided on a career in show business. I had a half hour program full of unicycle riding, tap dance, piano playing, singing, and sometimes, to give a sober touch of class, my Optimist Oration. I developed an unshakable sense of being part of a good dream.

The Act began when I joined Sandy McTavish's Ballet-Tap-Modern Dance clinic, and I quickly moved up from the chorus line to solo work, making my debut at the Heilig Theatre with "Airplane Roll":

"LOOK AND LISTEN"

> It was artistic love-at-first sight for Danny McCall and Peggy Darr when they met in Sandy Mctavish's dance studio two years ago. Now, they are one of the most sought-after entertainment attractions at clubs and schools (57 appearances last year); have won special honors as a team and singly. In fact, they could devote most of their time to their

bookings, if it weren't for school.

Their favorite duo number is "Casino de Paris," in which they are a junior-sized Fred Astaire and Ginger Rogers. Danny is slender, agile and blond. Peggy, a strawberry blonde, is petite, graceful, vivacious; toe-dances, as well as tap and novelty.

I asked them what they thought of while performing. Danny reports that he concentrates twenty-five percent on his performance and seventy-five percent on the audience. "If the audience doesn't look too enthusiastic I try to make easy steps look harder," he confides. Peggy remarks: "We just try harder."

Their future plans: Television.

—Glen Stadler, "Look and Listen,"
Eugene Register-Guard, March 17, 1953

And so it went: for the cops at the Safety Patrol Banquets, the Elks, Soroptimists, Masonic Temple, Kiwanis, Junior Chamber of Commerce, Churches, Odd Fellows, PTAs, Young Business Women, Lions, on and on while we drenched ourselves in movies where I was Donald O'Connor and Peg was Debbie Reynolds.

But I was really a single. I was always loaded down with equipment and props, and it was a royal pain dragging all that stuff around—my costumes, heavy wooden stairs I used for my "Stairway to Paradise" number, the tape-recorder with my piano accompaniment, the big suitcase I danced on for my "Round the World" sequence, the unicycle, and my huge doll, Ophelia Trundlebumps. Ophelia came into the world as a plain old red mop, but she'd been pillowed and gowned and gloved and braceleted by an Art Major at the U. of O. who painted a garish laughing face on her. Word of my talent got around, and I was invited to join the Journal Juniors, a talent show sponsored by the Portland *Journal*. There were about thirty of us kids, musicians, baton twirlers, dancers, singers, magicians. As usual I was the youngest and smallest. But I felt at home with them—the curly-headed trumpet player who did the dynamite solo in "One O'Clock Jump," the genius who could make whole symphonies on the piano out of random telephone numbers called out from the audiences, a boy who tap-danced on roller-skates, a fantastic "Tanglefoot" number, he was skinny as a rail and double-jointed all over like Ray Bolger. We were a Troupe, a Cavalcade, a Talent Caravan. Half-a-dozen times a year we'd pack into our chartered Greyhound and hit the road: to Corbett, Mt. Hood, to the Rain Festival in North Bonneville, to Multnomah Falls, Baker, Enterprise, Wallowa Lake, Pendleton, southward to Klamath Falls and Coos Bay. I couldn't do any one thing as well as the older kids could, but I had a ten minute spot where I did a little of everything. On my first trip, before anyone knew what I could do, I looked over the acrobats' unicycles and asked, "Is this so hard?" and they smiled, no, you think you're so smart, just ride one of 'em away—and I did. Man, I really annoyed those acrobats. The guys in the band were sneaky as hell; they smoked and even drank. The older girls thought I was darling. Sometimes they'd neck with me for harmless fun in the back of the bus or on beaches at night when we'd toast marshmallows and sing by the bonfire. Sometimes we'd play out under the stars in natural amphitheatres to audiences of two or three thousand. While the bus rolled on through the rain it was so beautiful to soul-kiss the fire-baton girl way in the back of the bus behind the costumes.

I wanted to live this way forever: getting on the Shasta Daylight in Eugene, going up to Portland for a tour, I'd check my suitcase full of tap-shoes and costumes and the huge garment bag containing Ophelia Trundlebumps; I'd pop peanuts into my mouth, the train would lurch, we were moving, and I'd wave to Mother and Dad until they were out of sight; I'd eat peanuts very slowly and wonder what new adventures in sex and show biz awaited me this time. The happiest moment of my life was late one night in Olympia, Washington—three acrobats and I did a unicycle square dance in the hotel parking lot, do-se-do on our one-wheels, pedaling in the gently falling snow, spinning to imaginary music, tears stinging my eyes.

In Eugene at Marjorie Caulkins' big Halloween come-as-you-are party, you had to wear whatever you were wearing when she invited you, and she had invited me right after a little program I did for the P.T.A. in the Roosevelt cafeteria. I was wearing my white suit and my patent-leather tap shoes. I hated the thought of the kids seeing me like that, in costume. I had studied, very carefully, what kind of clothes you had to wear to be popular, and I'd persuaded my parents to buy me all the right stuff—Strad shirts, Lord Jeff sweaters, pegged pants, English brogues. The idea was to be exactly like everybody else. Which was weird, given how hard I was working on the opposite.

Really, what were you supposed to do? It was so great to be a star, the focus of adoring eyes. To hear all the applause. Nothing could beat it. You were you. Totally you. But that made you a freak. A show-off. I tried to figure it out. What seemed to be involved here was the difference between adults and kids. Adults were easy. You tricked 'em. Adults were so simple, you just gave 'em what they wanted. And then they gave you what you wanted. But kids were complicated. With them I wasn't big enough, or strong enough, or something. How did you work it with kids your own age? The worst part was this: when you looked really closely, when you saw into it, you almost got the impression that the best thing to do was screw up, fail, get into trouble, have all sorts of problems, be stupid, make terrible mistakes—bingo! Everybody liked you. If you were lucky you had bad parents. Alcoholics were best; if your Mom or Dad was a booze-hound, you could get away with anything. But, to tell the truth, I didn't really like the popular kids. And that made me feel down on myself. I knew that I would do anything to get the respect of kids I didn't respect. And what did that make me?

The first two hours at the Halloween party I had fun. Marjorie had a crush on me, so we held hands, greeting everybody, laughing and talking. It was a "make-out" party: we turned off all the lights, and couples sat and lay together on couches and in big over-stuffed chairs, with Nat King Cole silky on the phonograph. Every hour we'd break for a few minutes; the girls would go off giggling upstairs and the guys'd huddle and tell how much they got. I hadn't got beans—ol' Marge wouldn't even open her mouth for tongues. All we did was kiss, for ten minutes at a time, lips sealed tight, each nose breathing.

The trouble started when Jerry found the Four Roses. Jerry passed the bottle around, and all the guys tried it—except, of course, me in my white suit and tap shoes. I had signed that "bargain" with my grandfather, after all, so even one sip would cost me a thousand smackeroos.

Jerry got totally smashed.

Then I made another fatal mistake. I wasn't one of the guys—and I wasn't a gentleman, either. Making out with Marjorie I was scared and a little angry; my left hand come up out of nowhere and landed on her right boob, and it was a fake bra, a really hard metal cup. Marjorie drew away with a shudder; her voice in the darkness said "Danny McCall!" so loud that all the other kids laughed.

And then we got raided. Nick Cerkoni and his tall buddy from Eugene High, Richie Green, crashed the party. They were smoking Chesterfields and carrying quart bottles of Hamm's. Cerkoni was the quarterback on our football team: tall and ruggedly handsome, way ahead of himself, he always hung out with older kids. I admired him enormously. And now my idol turned against me—he pantsed me! He and Richie Green got me by the arms and legs; Cerkoni undid my belt and Green pulled down my pants. They pulled my white pants clear off me. Those gunners dragged me kicking and screaming outside into the rain. And the girls saw everything—the girls saw Danny McCall in his white double-breasted suit coat which covered his private parts but not his skinny pink legs and black socks and tap shoes.

All alone, pantsed in the rain.

I looked around at everybody looking at me. Then I grabbed my soiled white trousers, and ran screaming into the night. I ran all the way home in the cold rain, and blew into our big white colonial house. Oh, whoops, I had totally forgotten. Mom and Dad were having a dinner party for the faculty of the U. of O. Speech and Drama Department. There was the rich cozy smell of one of Mother's banquets and all the professors and wives. I flew upstairs into my room and sat sobbing on my bed.

I cried so hard I woke up David. My little brother, five years old, came though the bathroom that connected our bedrooms and stood there in his white pj's, staring at me. I waved my hands for him to go away.

David stood there, sleepy, his head cocked to one side with his straw-blond hair and bright blue eyes.

He went down and got Dad.

My father came up and took me into the little bathroom. He sat on the toilet and I sat on the edge of the tub. He held my hands. He listened to my breathless story. Then, softly, he said, "Go back."

"No," I said. I could do almost anything but that—"NO!"

He said, "You have to go back." His hazel eyes looked into my hazel eyes. I was his son, and he loved me, and he was the boss of all those people downstairs whose laughter and talk floated up to us.

So I did what my Dad said. I put on my wadded-up

white pants. I washed my face. I walked slowly back to the party. Returning to the scene of the crime. When I got there, Cerkoni was surprised. He looked at me, hard, but he didn't give me any more trouble. And I had a pretty good time.

Before the party broke up at midnight the girls were suddenly laughing hysterically and really fussing over something, making a big deal out of it. Finally I saw it, and it certainly was a big deal: a photograph of Richie Green standing with his hands on his hips, a goofy smile on his face, his pants down around his knees and his big dong hanging out. Aghast, I looked across the living room at Richie sitting there drinking beer and laughing. He knew his dick was being stared at and passed around among the girls, and he didn't give a shit, he actually enjoyed it. I'd made such a cry-baby fool of myself about just being pantsed. Well, maybe it was an entirely different matter if your weenie was a log like that. Lately my own little dinger has begun to act up, especially in Ross Poston's attic when we looked over his Dad's *Sunshine and Health* magazines. But I just had peach fuzz. Richie Green's giant python came out of a dark jungle. Where would a photograph like that have come from?—there wasn't a camera shop in Eugene that would develop it. In the kitchen girls were trying to pour coffee into Jerry, but as soon as the coffee went down it'd come right back up again, all over the linoleum. What a night! I hardly knew what to think. Walking home in the rain I realized I was crying. But it was different this time. I wasn't really unhappy. Just tired, I guess. The world was so *mysterious*.

When my parents were at a small party somewhere, I was charged with holding down the fort and watching David. He was six and I was thirteen, just the two of us in our big house in Eugene. We used to play slipper tag, after bath, and David my little brother was always It, trundling along in his little red and black plaid robe. I had a pair of floppy slipper-sox, inch-thick foam rubber soles. With all the lights turned off, I would take the flashlight and roam around the house; I'd wait and wait and sneak up behind him Hee-Hee-Hee and belt him in the head with one of those foam rubbery slipper-sox. The flashlight beam jerks, jagged, zig-zagging on the walls and ceiling.

When mother and father got home, and David showed them the red handprint on his ass, father was sad and told me it was not my business to discipline my brother. I was never to spank David. I knew what to do the next time we were alone. I put the pillow on his face, then I lay across the pillow. David wriggling and kicking and jerking his legs, scratching frantically with his tiny arms—Never Spank Your Brother (I'm Not! I'm Not!) and when I pulled off the very small, fine beautiful face was convulsed in silent screams. For ten seconds, no sound: just the lips round and wide like a purple bowl-rim, his lungs locked.

Growing out of babyhood David had begun to wonder what shadows were. I had flung a pair of corduroy pants on the closet door: the shadow of the pants on the wall. David turned his vast blue eyes up, and said, "Pants on the wall?" He said it again to himself, "Pants on the wall."

One night Mom and Dad deposited us at the movie

theatre for the evening show. David in that brown jacket with the furry collar, we were high up in the balcony and Cerkoni and Green were behind us, in the last row, necking with their girls. Father said I was not to let David go to the bathroom alone, I had to go with him, and right in the middle of the best part of the movie, David had to go. I refused. I dug my nails into his wrist halfway between the heel of the hand and the elbow and growled, *"Don't cry, don't you cry, don't you embarrass me in front of Cerkoni,"* and David was desperately trying to keep it in, not make a sound, Cerkoni and Green necking with the girls behind us and David's lips hugely screaming and blue, white light on purple lips.

In the V.F.W. Hall in 1953 the scrawled graffiti over the urinal said

> Don't Look Up Here For A Laugh —
> The Joke's In Your Hand!

I couldn't bear to think I was anything "short" of a miracle. I sure didn't seem to be.

Late at night I'd lock myself in my room with the tape recorder, and put on my own special spool of tape. When I was sure Mom and Dad were asleep, I'd get all naked in my bed, my flashlight trained on the Playmate of the Month that I folded out across the pillow. I studied and loved every inch of her. I spoke to her into the mike. I'd talk over the details of my day with her, my fears and my joys, and she loved me because I told her so sincerely. There in the dark with my flash and mike, I had to be careful.

I'd whisper into the mike: "Don't be ashamed now, don't—don't turn your head away," I was gentle but firm. "Look at me now, look at your true love, and I'd show her

>Danny McCall's Living Penis!

Then I would disconnect the mike, re-wind, put it on "play" and do the scene silently all over again, turning the flashlight from my Playmate's body to mine as my recorded voice came on like the sound-track to our perfect movie.

In concert choir some altos were giggling about a small first tenor with pimples who used a warmed cantaloupe, and I said sardonically that for him a pitted olive would do—and those girls laughed and quoted me for days, but—how *do* you do it? I lay in bed in the dark with my big stiff thing, the flashlight trained on it, and I just didn't know what I was supposed to do. I knocked the playmate under the bed and lay there until things calmed down and I could put on my pajama pants again.

Sometimes, in the middle of the night, it would happen. I'd have to get up and go into the bathroom and wipe it off with toilet paper. I thought the final thing happened only in your sleep.

If there was just someone I could ask.

On Portland's Channel 13 (Television Diablo) "Stairway to Stardom" talent show every Sunday afternoon, first prize was a pair of round-trip airplane tickets to Hawaii. In Eugene I watched eagerly and wrote in for an audition; they sent back a postcard with a time and instructions to bring your own "music and props, if any." Mother and Dad drove me over to Portland, the backseat full of unicycle, costume, and Ophelia Trundlebumps.

The TV Diablo studios were drab and disappointing: small, dusty, crowded with accordion players, trumpet soloists, steel guitar cowboys and cowgirls, greasy crooners ("Unchained Melody," "Tennessee Waltz," "Let Me Go, Lover"), a ventriloquist, ballerinas ("Afternoon of a Fawn," "Etudes"), and mothers who couldn't get sitters and brought along the babies. You had to wait, and wait, before you even got into the next line in a darker room where the cameras and piano were.

Each week's winner was decided by the number of votes mailed to the station. I was afraid the friends of other contestants might send in dozens of cards each, it wouldn't be fair, so I made a general announcement at a Roosevelt pep rally, making a joke out of it. But when the station called me the next week, they said my votes came in from everywhere.

Then I had to wait three Sundays for the finals when all the weekly winners would compete for the trip to Hawaii. The only one I was worried about was a skinny guy, a music director at a Church in Tracy, who played lullabies on drinking glasses, rubbing his wet finger around the edges.

For the final round, which was being judged by three TV personalities in San Francisco, I did my "Globetrotter," rolling in on my unicycle, and then hopping off to play piano and sing "When Irish Eyes Are Smiling," dipping down to Spain where I picked up Ophelia and sang "Lady of Spain" to her—in Spanish—up to Moscow for my Russian dance steps, bouncing all over the globe and ending up back state-side with my big wooden suitcase to hop onto and kick off from, a furious final tap to "Stars And Stripes Forever."

Next afternoon on the front page of the Eugene *Register-Guard*:

DANNY McCALL WINS BIG
TRIP TO SAILORS' UTOPIA

There had been some loose talk about "all expenses paid," but the prize finally turned out to be just two airfares. So Dad had to shell out for two more, and the hotel rooms, a rent-a-car, meals, and a guided tour of the big island. It was like when the Optimists had paid for my trip to Louisville but Dad had to come through for Mother's fare. So now, as we sat at the elegant table at Volcano House and saw the prices on the menu, Dad muttered, "Keep on winning, son, and you'll bankrupt the family!"

On Waikiki, David was happy as a clam digging away on the beach, and I took my first surfing lesson from my chunky brown instructor. He told me to try to ride the first wave in lying down on the board. But after the first ten yards I got to my knees, then to my feet, and I stood there looking at Diamond Head, hearing my beach-boy hollering encouragement, then I stood on one leg—Didn't ride that unicycle for nothing!—stood in the spray and the golden sunshine, slicing in the curl, singing, oh singing, yelling, "Lady of Spain, I adore you," as the coral and green water came racing under me.

CHAPTER FOUR

THE MODESTO KID

"In writing a book like this, it is necessary to face one of the least appealing figures to have traversed the earth's crust—that is, one's high school self."
— Mark Edmunson, *Teacher*

"God, it would be good to be a fake somebody rather than a real nobody."
— Mike Tyson

"But what can a decent man speak of with most pleasure?
Answer: Of himself.
Well, so I will talk of myself."
— Fyodor Dostoyevsky,
Notes From the Underground

1954-1957, Modesto, California

In late 1953 Dad was one of the candidates for the Presidency of Modesto Junior College. Over the Christmas holidays he went down to California for an interview. Then the family waited. And finally one spring day in Eugene when I came in from playing catch with David, Dad had just hung up the phone in his study. His hand still on it, he looked at me and said, "Go ask your Mother if she wants to move to Modesto."

She did.

But approaching it in our white Cadillac that summer of '54, the McCalls were not impressed: dusty miles of scrubby vineyards to all horizons on both sides of the highway, beat-up little country stores, junkyards, empty Drive-Ins. Modesto was a "Valley town." Anyone coming from Sacramento or San Francisco had to pass through it on the way to Yosemite. Eugene had been green, deeply green, with buttes and bluffs and hills and forests, the sparkling Willamette and McKenzie rivers that Dad loved to fish in (while Mom and I waited in the car playing Honeymoon Bridge). Modesto was flat as a pancake and the color of straw. The little house that had been rented for us on North Olive Street had a dilapidated back porch, and the scruffy man who lived in the adjoining apartment parked his liquor-store truck right in front. It wasn't at all a "President's residence."

That summer I stayed close to two sons, John and Richard, of the superintendent of schools. They took me swimming at beautiful pools in the yards of fine homes. Wealth was a Good Christian Life.

John and Richard took me to a party one night, another rich house, and all the guys gathered at the radio to listen to the Charles-Marciano fight. I asked one boy in a lime cashmere who he was rooting for, and when he said, "You can't root for a wop, but you sure as hell can't root for a nigger"—it shocked me. All of them would go to Downey High School, and I was relieved when it was decided I would go to Modesto High.

By my sophomore year the Contests were coming almost every weekend. Mother registered me in the American Legion Oratory Contest and I thought I was going all the way again—then I took a third, a *third* in the California Finals in L.A. After the contest one of the judges said to me, "You really wrap yourself in the flag, son," and then I had to drive 400 miles in a station wagon back to Modesto with my 3 Legionnaire sponsors; I wanted to take a plane—anything, anything —just not 10 hours in the backseat a loser.

But those were accidents, the sophomore jinx. I only include them to make me seem human.

Reader, you are right, "I only include…" is a bad sentence, a cheap shot, a tonal failure. O, reader, I do see how hard it is for you. I'm afraid I really am telling you this story the way it has to be told, and I quite accept it if you say, "You've made your point. But surely that point could be made in a very few pages." Do not understand me too quickly; I have other points in mind. You see, I don't at all dislike the boy. He didn't know it was bullshit and he knew damn well it was; you miss my meaning if you think otherwise. Why on earth should he have—could he have—put his foot down? He's going to get a lot more "screwed up," if you wish, but let us, after all, be serious. This is an amazing country.

In September and October at Modesto High School I was anonymous and miserable. Between Christmas '53 and Fall '54 I had grown seven inches, from 5'4" to 5'11", my pubic hair came in, and my voice changed. But I didn't have the right clothes, and when I'd try to be witty in Geometry or Spanish I'd just get nasty glances. The girls didn't like me. And a big pimply Future Farmer of America started some Cerkoni stuff, would bump me in the hall, towel-snapping me after showers in gym. I was lost.

The breakthrough seemed to come one Friday afternoon. The pep rallies at Modesto High were always frantic, hundreds of kids filling the auditorium for songs and speeches and the introduction of the football team, more songs and speeches, and then the school hymn at the end. Our skit for the Lodi game began with a little take-off on the *George Gobel Show*, the hit of the year; everybody went all to pieces if you just said "You can't hardly get them no more" or "Well I'll be a dirty bird." I could do a perfect imitation of George Gobel. Feeling outcast and stupid, I'd been glued to the TV every night, staying up late, alone, watching the Steve Allen's *Tonight Show* from New York. We hadn't had TV in Eugene, and now I couldn't get enough of it.

At the pep rally I was supposed to introduce the skit, a couple of sentences. I stepped out onto the stage at a quarter to three. It was all dark in the huge auditorium. I felt lonely and frightened. I told my first joke, and there were some giggles, and then I was George Gobel for a minute, and that got a nice laugh. I told a few jokes stolen from Steve Allen—*All that TV I watched by myself while you guys were out having sex parties!!*—and the laughter was building, for a moment I thought they might be laughing at me. I paused and walked down in front of the footlights, and scratched my head—no, no, it was okay, they were really enjoying it—so I did a brief sketch making fun of the recent hit movie, *Shane*. I was bewildered little Brandon deWilde whining, "Shane? – *Shane*?—and then asking, "Is this *your* gun, Shane?"— and accidentally blowing Alan Ladd's head off—I stared down at his corpse, "Hey, uh, *Jeez*—SHANE?"

The whole auditorium exploded in laughter. Standing there in front of the footlights I could see their faces now, and they were all laughing *with* me, yes, oh yes, and standing on the apron of the stage I could see the three rows in the center down front, the football team in their jackets. I started joshing with the team, I did a routine about their breaking training and drinking too much beer: "But, Coach, I fell asleep the minute my head hit the lawn." The lettermen were nudging each other and slapping their legs.

I did a brief version of Victor Borge's "Phonetic Punctuation," Dad had got a phonograph record of it in Eugene, and played it a lot for guests, Dad just loved it. So I'd learned how to do all the funny noises of phonetic punctuation to zip through the legend of Lady Eleanor and Sir Henry with all the blopz-zit plurr-dnk:

> O flip my darling flip how long has it been since I was at your side screeqq?
> She replied pilf (she was left-handed) I only
> Fear for the future zzzzztd.

The sound for a period was like a cork coming out

of a bottle, only messier, and when I finished—"The only sound was that of Sir Henry's departing horse"—I put in the period, and the auditorium went bananas. I'd done it dozens of times, and there was always that big laugh, but this was the first time I got the joke: Sir Henry's horse had—*farted*. Phonetic Punctuation! The sound of a departing horse was the sound of a departing fart, and on the Modesto High stage I buckled over in helpless laughter because I had taken so long to get my own joke.

But despite my success at the pep rally, I couldn't seem to make any friends. One girl told me that I seemed "above it all," that I suffered from a "Star Complex."

So I was delighted—and a bit confused—when Frank Brasil asked me to come to his hayride. Brasil wasn't very big, but he was powerful: a fullback on the "B" team and the Northern California Lightweight Wrestling champion. In Concert Choir he could lift one end of the piano way up off the floor. Frank was terrific at the Bop Dances in Legion Hall; he'd strut stiff-legged, pawing the floor with his desert boot like a bull.

Frank even picked me up—in an old black Buick Roadmaster that he'd been working on. I couldn't figure out why he'd include me in his hayride, and he did make a remark, "I don't know if you associate socially with Portagees." But his sister Carla was coming home from her freshman year at San Francisco State, and she and I had made out once on the ski bus to dodge Ridge. So I'd be her escort.

We plowed out toward the Brasil ranch on the road to Tracy, that Buick could really move. He was drinking

Gallo wine and passed me the bottle. I almost told him I couldn't, and then I saw my way out: I held the bottle up, pretended to take a big swig, but held my tongue in the hole so I didn't get any at all. I did have to refuse the Chesterfields—but that worked out okay; he said, "Oh yeah, you're on the swim team."

When we got out to the ranch he asked me to help rub down the horses. My horse's name was Tequila; I stroked his nose, "Easy, boy," and Frank laughed, "McCall, you're such a clown, that's a mare." Frank looked at my slacks, and said, "Shoulda told you to wear Levi's." I didn't tell him I had never owned a pair.

It was a quarter to eight and I wondered where all the kids were for the party. Frank said his sister might be back by now. We talked a little about her. He said Carla always liked me. His own "filly" was Juanita Silva, he said he was thinking about marrying her. "Women are pissers, right, Dan?"

I nodded, holding Tequila's reins.

"They sure fuck up your life-plan."

"Yep."

We walked our horses through a little creek and up a hill. He pointed out their property and said it was all going to be his someday. There was a nice ground fog; it wasn't chilly, just mysterious.

When we were done silently walking our horses through the ground fog, we went into the house for Beam and Hamm's. He had to piss and I poured my booze down the sink. I held some of the beer in my mouth for a while so it would be on my breath.

Carla came in, driving her old plastic-boat Corvette. She had notebooks with "S.F. State" decals on them.

She seemed glad to see me and I looked at her navy sweatshirt and remembered suddenly how flat-chested she was and how I'd felt the mole above her left nipple on the ski bus. She had "rye and ginger" and we talked about Drama. She had a little role in *Orpheus Descending*, by Tennessee Williams. Frank sat there watching us talk, his cowboy boots propped up and crossed on the seat of a kitchen chair.

Then everybody started showing up, in big cars and pick-up trucks. It was a real Portagee crowd—I knew a lot of them from Choir, but I was a little nervous about some of the guys in their Future Farmers of America blue cord jackets—they were passing around bottles and smoking. I wondered if they got drunk if they might pants me, like Cerkoni in Eugene. I tried to be casual, and held a cigarette.

I thought the horses would pull the hay-wagon, but it was a truck. Carla was really putting away that rye and ginger. We sat at the back, in the hay and ground fog, and every once in a while she'd call out to one of her Dee-Gee sisters. She had on a lot of perfume, and I liked her long black hair. At one point she said, "I really was kidding, that time, about your build."

I'd forgotten about that.

"In a few years I know it'll be terrific."

I smiled.

"You're a lot nicer make-out than you think."

"Really?"

"You're just afraid to keep it sincere."

I nodded.

She let me put my arm around her and brush my hand against her breast.

"I don't think I'll ever forget my first impression of you," she said. "I guess you know I couldn't stand you."

The clouds against the moon were melancholy, spacious. One couple got off the wagon and went off into the trees—others called to them, "Don't do anything we wouldn't do."

"But then I did a lot of thinking," she went on, and I began to realize exactly what you're like—and —" she looked up at me, whispering, "I like it."

I kissed her. She really smelled of that perfume and the rye and ginger. Her tongue leapt in and I sucked on it. She knew how to do it. We lay back in the hay, and I nuzzled her wonderful hair.

She said, "I guess there's no subtle way of saying what you can't even say teasingly—anyway, what you don't have in build, you sure make up for in personality."

We were stuck in a little gully, and everybody had to get off the wagon. I joined the guys, we pushed and heaved, and then we were okay again. I really liked that—the truck whining away, digging for traction, and all of us males at the rear putting our backs into it.

Carla and I, casually together.

We stopped in a clearing. There was wood for a bonfire and Frank was lighting it, dousing it all with fuel. He threw in a match, it exploded, and everybody whooped.

I held her hand. "Shall we wander away for a while?"

She looked at me and stared into my eyes for a long time. The Portagee bonfire was exciting on her cheeks. She held back her head, let the dark hair fall on her sweatshirt, and said, "Yes."

We walked through that beautiful ground fog. She

said, "Promise me one thing, Dan. Please continue to be the way you are as long as you possibly can."

We walked in dark places. It was damp, incredibly real, and the voices of the party trailed away behind us.

Carla said, "Will it be a long time before you forget me?"

I started to nod—and then I said I never would.

We walked.

Just as we could see the bonfire ahead, she stopped, and turned me to her. "You're going to make it in Hollywood, I just know it, Danny. You've got talent to burn."

I stopped. "I—I love you." But then I heard my words, and I caught myself. "Wait a minute, I don't know you well enough to say that, I mean it isn't right to—"

She put her little fingers to my mouth. "Hush."

At the end, outside the barn, we dawdled together. She said, "I hope you'll always be as successful as you are now."

I felt bad. I said, "You know, about that 'I love you'—I shouldn't have —"

And this time she didn't hush me with her hand. She shook her head, the long black hair swaying, and stopped my words with her lips, tenderly. "May all your sweetest dreams come true, Danny."

Waiting around out there for Frank, wondering if he would drive me home or if I should try to get a lift from somebody or if I would have to call Dad, I fell around in the loft of their barn. I felt wonderful, did little two steps with a memory of Peggy Darr, and fell at length like Donald O'Connor in the hay. This night could be the real turning point in my life: *I will be invited again*. I am successful, not show-offy, just *one of them* at a party. With the guys 'n gals. I could hear girls on the phone—oh, yes, we *have* to have Danny McCall. He's always there. And at the next one I'll drink beer... really... I will actually get drunk, I'll polish off a six-pack of Hamm's the Beer Refreshing, and the guys'll carry me home

> show me the way to go home
> I'm tired and I wanna go to bed

and the folks will be frantic and sad but respectable of course, as long as the guys are there and jolly at the door—but then the door will be closed, and Mother will weep and Dad will be vastly disappointed in his stern quiet way.

Alone, leaning back on the ladder in the Brasil's dark barn, I decided that if I came home really *drunk*, they'd have to *do* something. Perhaps I would have to compose a letter to Gramps telling him I hadn't kept "my part" of our "bargain." At the least they could "ground" me for a month, that happens to a lot of kids. And Frank can come over sometimes in the evening, just to keep me company and "shoot the shit." I'll let him smoke in my room, I'll even buy cigarettes to have on hand if he runs out. And at the right time I'll casually ask him about sex, I'll say quietly, "there must be something more," and then I'll listen closely to what he says.

When Frank drove me home I was frightened; he was quite drunk and we fishtailed all over the road at 90. He seemed very interested in how it went with Carla and me, and kept trying to get me to finish the bottle of Beam. I said I was "ridin' high," and I had work to do in the morning. He muttered something about milkin' with a hangover, and I said I thought cows were milked in the late afternoon and he said "Fuckin' A." But then I wasn't sure if he'd even heard me, and I was nervous about our being in the left lane.

When we pulled up on Trinity, he banged the lights off and cut the motor. "I'll tell you the truth, Dan, I'm worried about my sister. She's over there in 'Frisco, all that college and drama—you should see the guy she's going out with."

I looked in and saw the lamp in the family room.

"Can I talk to you straight, Dan?"

"Yes."

He took a drag on the cigarette, and finished the bottle himself. "He's a jig, Dan—a goddamn jig."

I shook my head.

"I don't know how you feel about it, but I—I'm responsible now. I hate to see that kind of thing goin' on anyway, and when it's your own sister. You understand."

"Of course."

He rolled down the window and popped his ash out. I hoped the folks weren't watching.

He looked at our house. "That's a nice place."

We sat there.

At length, Frank said, "Women are real pissers, Dan. Juanita and me, I don't know. When you got to get your rocks off, you'll do anything. You'll promise them the goddamn moon."

I said, again, I knew.

He gathered himself, whacked me on the thigh. "You take care—don't be a stranger."

But after that night, whenever I tried to talk or joke with him in the hall, he seemed cold. Maybe it was because I never called Carla again. But it would have been a mistake. Father told me that some women could "ruin you," it doesn't matter who throws the mud, it still sticks on you, and your whole life would be beyond repair.

By January of 1956 I was old enough to get my driver's license, and driving home one night from *Rebel Without a Cause* I wanted to be mixed-up and cool like James Dean and have the folks terrified that they couldn't "get through" to their Danny. I went out and recklessly drove a few miles at 100, taking one long last final skid-drift onto a canal bank, almost losing control, like the scene with the cars on the cliff. Beside the black water of the irrigation ditch I relived every scene in the movie, gathering power and despair. I imagined being drunk in the police station, a friend to poor Sal Mineo, quietly intense with Natalie Wood. When at last I came home after midnight they were sick with worry, telling me how they almost called the police, the movie was over at 9. I loved it. Actually thinking about calling the police. And, taking Dad's lecture sullenly, patiently, pacing my room like a caged animal, I suddenly slammed my fist on the side of the TV: "I saw it twice, I saw the *second* show, did you ever consider that?" It was a lie, but it floored them. Why don't you let me be myself, why won't you leave me alone?" That hit. It was the moment of truth. "Can't you see?—you're tearing me apart. You've given me everything except one thing, the thing I want most—you don't trust me!" Dad's mouth was open a little, his eyes gone gray; Mother was in shock. They were helpless and I slammed the wall with my forehead. I stormed into the bathroom, slammed the door, and watched myself in the mirror. I was James Dean.

After things calmed down a bit Dad went off to bed. I went into the kitchen to make a toasted cheese sandwich.

Mom was still up, standing there. "You do realize what time it is?"

I looked at my watch. Finally I said, "I'm sorry, I didn't think you guys would worry so much."

"Oh Danny." She looked so disappointed in me.

The sink was white, deep. I bent into it.

"You'll burn your sandwich." She moved quickly and opened the grille.

I ate, standing, looking out at the moon.

"Tell me what's wrong, darling."

"Nothing. Nothing's wrong."

I turned to her. "What I mean is, everything's okay, except I don't have any friends."

Mother moved slightly, standing there in her robe. "Oh, Danny, no boy in Modesto is so admired, so looked up to, as you."

And I could hear her getting ready to go on with the thing she always said when I was younger, in Eugene, when I was worried about not being invited to the in-group parties—she kept telling me they didn't invite me because they were "jealous"—and I didn't want to hear it anymore.

"Danny, you could have all the friends you want,

just for the asking."

I thought about that, staring into the sink. *Why don't I ask?* It seemed funny, and I ducked my head under the faucet for a drink. I said into the funnel of water, gurgling, "Will ggyou be my frreeggnd?" I pulled out and wiped my mouth on my sleeve.

She didn't say anything.

I went out into the garage and for a laugh I brought Ophelia in from the Caddy. I stood with her. I tried to smooth things over and be casual, but Ophelia fell down, skidded onto the linoleum like a corpse. For a moment I tried to pretend it didn't mean anything, it was like dropping a newspaper that you were through reading, but then I saw that I couldn't do that and stumbled down over Ophelia's scarlet hem, trying to pick her up. Mother had a tear in her eye. "It's all right," I muttered, "here, I've got her now, it's all right."

"Nothing's wrong," I said. "Truly." I so wished that I hadn't said anything.

The next morning we all pretended as if nothing had happened.

Each year the National Forensic League Finals were held at the University of San Francisco. I figured I'd try "Dramatic Interp"—I remembered that big theatre Dad had built at the U. of O. and the remarkable production of *Death of a Salesman* that inaugurated it, that great guy who did Biff Loman. I got the text of the play out of the Modesto Public Library, and Mom and I cut a ten-minute reading out of it. We zeroed in on the fireworks between father and son:

> *Biff:* I never got anywhere because you blew me so full of hot air I could never stand taking orders from anybody! That's whose fault it is.

It was dangerous stuff. I thought of the Optimist Contest—is that what Dad did, he blew me full of hot air? For several evenings I stood in their bedroom at the foot of their four-poster, gradually memorizing the words and getting the feel of it. Mom lay in bed coaching me. Mother lay there in a big bank of pillows, coaxing me to the deep heart of the tragedy:

> *Biff:* Pop, I ran down eleven flights with a pen in my hand today. And suddenly I stopped, you hear me? And in the middle of that office building, do you hear this? I stopped in the middle of that building and I saw—the sky. I saw the things that I love in this world.

Mom swept her arms out in that frilly blue bedjacket, getting the intonations right: "and I saw—the sky. I saw the things that I *love* in this world." Then I'd do it, exactly the way she did it, we'd do it together:

> *Biff:* And I looked at the pen and said to myself, what the hell am I grabbing this for? Why am I trying to become what I don't want to be? Pop! I'm a dime a dozen, and so are you!
> *Willy:* I am not a dime a dozen! I am Willy Loman, and you are Biff Loman!

I had to do a few words of Willy (the rules for the contest said you had to do a minimum of three voices), and I pitched Willy at a low, bewildered whisper. Mom had me moan the feeling behind it—and it just killed me to see everything going to pieces between the baffled father and the lonely, thwarted son. I cried out Arthur Miller's words:

> *Biff:* I'm not bringing home any prizes any more, and you're going to stop waiting for me to bring them home!

Oh, *Lord*. I stopped and looked at Mom in bed.

Suddenly another expression came into her eyes, she was distracted, she looked *worried*—but just for a second.

She winked.

Gradually it began to come round, the waves of rage and tenderness. *Concentrate*, Mom said. Concentrate, first, on yourself. Concentrate on everything you've got to say and do, until it all becomes second nature. Then concentrate (without looking at them) on your audience. In Oratory you have to stare down the crowd; in Drama you have to *sense* them, blind, and listen to the nuances of their silent attention. You have to be able to pull them with you, bring them out of their chairs and up into the middle of this heart-breaking stand-off between father and son.

Every night Dad would come in late, weary from another meeting at MJC—the college was entering an era of rapid expansion, and he was presiding over a huge building program, new Ag buildings, new bookstore,

Science labs, Library. Exhausted, Dad would slump in the big green rocking chair, and listen to Mom and me working out the tragedy. Dad helped me with the very end, the catch in the throat, as Willy Loman turns from his son ("What are you doing? What are you doing?") to his wife ("Why is he crying?"). That, we decided, was where we'd leave it. I choked back a sob, my hands tense trembling in the air: "Why is he crying?" I held it there, lost, totally lost, nothing going right, my whole life wasted, all my hopes for my son dying in me. I was *stricken*—I looked at the bright attentive eyes of my parents.

Dad said, sighing, "Well, if that doesn't win, I don't know a damn thing about Speech."

Mom nodded: "It's strong—yes, it's very strong."

The bus didn't get back to Modesto until after midnight, Sunday. The MHS Student Body President drove me home to North Olive. Mom and Dad were waiting up, and I said I lost—I lurched into the house and said I lost in the preliminary rounds, it was all a big *gyp*, I just wanted to hit the hay and sleep it off. I was crushed, and I closed my bedroom door behind me. Then I unwrapped the mighty gold trophy from my raincoat (it was too long to fit into my suitcase), and put it on my desk, this tall beauty with the mahogany base and the over-arching gold laurel wreaths. Mom and Dad were padding about out there, whispering, as if there'd been a death in the family. Finally I took pity on them. I turned my desk lamp as a spotlight on the trophy, jumped under the covers, and called out like a forlorn widdle boy: "Could somebody kiss a loser goodnight?"

They came in, and saw, and went crazy. We stayed up another hour while I told them everything. The struggle between Willy and Biff, well, it tore everybody's heart out. Mom cried; Dad said there's nothing's like that feeling you get when you got 'em all in the palm of your hand.

It was two o'clock before we turned in. I lay in the darkness—"Optimism for Courageous Living" and *Death of a Salesman*. Sunshine and Midnight—what a combination!

At dawn, in my dream, I was Biff Loman with a pen in my hand, tearing along on a unicycle on a surfboard.

I did have a new girlfriend—Julie—and I taught her how to ski at Dodge Ridge; coming home on the chartered Greyhounds it was like the old Eugene days and Julie was the fire-baton girl. Dad said it was okay to take the Cad around the neighborhood, and Julie lived just six blocks away, we drove around a lot after school and evenings, we'd lie down and mess around. We went farther and farther. I took a major step: I bought a rubber. I thought about it for days, practiced speeches, picked out a drugstore where I was sure I would not be known, walked around it a long time, burst right in, I knew the druggist would have stepped out for coffee and there'd be a woman, but no, it was okay, it was a man, and when I told him what I wanted he just asked "How many?"

Well... I've only got one....

He explained that they came in packs of a dozen or tins of three. I said a tin. I got into the folks' white Cadillac and drove out on a canal bank and tried to put one of them on, but it seemed that you had to be stiff and straight before you could do it, so I blew it up like a balloon. Then I had trouble getting it properly rolled again. So I blew it back up, tied a knot at the base, and set it on the canal; it bobbed away. Now I had two.

One night after a movie, Julie and I went out to that deserted spot on the canal bank. The car radio was on, and suddenly I heard it for the first time:

> Since my baby left me,
> I've found a new place to dwell,
> down at the end of Lonely Street
> it's called Heartbreak Hotel.

Julie and I took off all our clothes, in the front seat, and we made out all over our bodies, got so excited we could barely breathe, and her boobs and her pussy were so sweet, she was touching me in ways I'd never even considered—it was *wonderful*—and then, suddenly, she wanted to go swimming.

What? Well, okay.

We walked hand in hand to the edge of the water and I dove in. Julie was walking toward me, her breasts bobbing on the black water. She put her arms around me—and then—her legs! Her legs around me under the water! And my penis shot up.

She giggled. "Who's that knocking at my door?"

There was a dam ahead, and the water deepened out to a real old-fashioned swimmin' hole. We separated and swam, played a little blind tag, gurgling and rolling, and she was making yummy noises.

I went underwater, hollered loud and beat my

stomach with my fists.

We dried off with her navy sweatshirt and my tee-shirt which I threw up into a walnut tree, spread out. I liked the beauty mark on her breast very much, and she let me put my lips on it. Then I announced that I had "protection."

She wasn't sure.

I said, "I don't want you to be—frightened."

"Oh no," she said, kind of fast, "it's not that. And —" she cutely ducked her head, "I don't want you to think I'm a prick-teaser."

So we lay there together again, and I started with one finger, then moved to two, and she was squeezing me, pulling on me so hard I thought she'd tear the thing off, and she was moaning, her back arching, "Oh—*now, now*," and I didn't know if I was supposed to get the rubber or what. She was really hurting hell out of my rod, but I didn't want to let her down, so I said, "Me too, yes, now now," when two headlights came down the deserted road on the canal bank, and then we really had to *move it*, Julie and I, we were in trouble, and there just wasn't time to go for the tee-shirt in the walnut tree, it was all we could do to get what was close at hand, those headlights coming at us like God's eyes—oh *why* did I take the keys out of the ignition?—and then we were off in the Caddy, Julie rushing into her clothes and me still bare-assed, driving so fast to get away, Christ, I almost drove straight into the dam, that's cool, and I was up to 60 by the County Road, and wondering what I'd say when the fuzz stopped me for speeding and I was naked—Julie was yelling at me, like it was my fault or something, why the hell was she mad at me?, and she kept giving me lectures while I put my clothes on, and kept *on* giving me lectures, she said she would never be in that "position" again, and—

We got onto 10th Street and dragged up and down it a few times. When we ran into her brother, Tony, she opened the door of the Cad, and ran to Tony's Plymouth.

I dragged 10th a few more times myself, and then Tony stopped me down by the bus depot and said what-the-hell-is-this-all-about? And I don't know what possessed me—*Whatever* was I thinking? How could anybody in the world be so *stupid?*—I showed him the two rubbers in my wallet.

He looked at me for a long time. He was a big guy. He said, "You wait right here, McCall." He went back to his car. I could see Ron sitting over there talking to Julie. Tony and Ron were both on the football team. They had me boxed in at Burgie's Drive-In. Tony came back over and pulled me out of the open car door before I could lock it. "I warned you," he said, and hit me a good one. I was smiling, hoping those damn tears wouldn't come, still smiling.

"Wipe it off."

Slam! Tony was hitting me on the arms and shoulders.

"Wipe it off, you little shit."

"No."

Slam!

Then Ron came over and hit me a couple of times. It wasn't hurting too terribly much so I didn't stop smiling. You can kill me, but I won't wipe off my smile. Horns were honking, and people were gunning their cars in neutral.

My smile weakened, flickered, and then the oddest thing happened.

Three hairy-ass-busters on big motorcycles pulled up in a shower of noise between the cars. Out of a nightmare, these three, raunchy beasts with chains and Levi jackets cut off at the armpits. The head man with Elvis Presley ducktails did a wheel-stand, then killed it, got off and muscled toward us. He looked at Tony and Ron. He looked at me. "Need any help, kid?"

These nightmare men, the ones who were going to kill me one day, these Cerkoni Ghouls, they—they wanted to *help* me?

Tony and Ron backed off a little. Tony said, "He screwed my sister."

I started to say No, No I didn't, I never did it with anybody, I want to, I really want to, to know what it's like, but I *didn't*.

The Monster smiled at me. "How was she?" Then he glared at Tony.

What?! *Je*-sus, *what*?! I simply did not know what to say. People were getting out of their cars, gathering to watch.

Tony and Ron hesitated, then retreated back into their car with Julie, and they peeled off.

"Thanks," I said to the gang.

"All right, brother."

What? What did he call me?

Monster Man walked back to his bike and gave the finger to some kid who was honking.

I went into Burgie's for a Coke. I felt confused. Oh well, I was just happy to have my clothes on.

CHAPTER FIVE

THE CONFESSIONS OF JOHNNY APPLESEED

"I've learned that what's better than applause is that profound silence of someone listening to you. That is the best."
— Avon Long

"Johnny Appleseed was never a boaster at all. In life he had been John Chapman (1775-1847), a New England Swedenborgian who had conceived it to be his mission to sow fruit trees through the Middle West, and had spent nearly half a century traveling by canoe and on foot, reading aloud from the Bible and leaving orchards behind him… After his death he became a frontier saint, almost a god of fertility."
— F.O. Matthiessen, *American Renaissance*

"The profoundest lessons are not the lessons of reason; they are sudden strains that permanently warp the mind."
— *The Education of Henry Adams*

September 1956, Modesto

"Johnny Appleseed" was the only one I did for my contemporaries, the other kids, the only one in which I wanted to be loved for something we all love. "Johnny Appleseed" wasn't like any of the others in which I was Dad's little Robbie the Robot. This one was all mine, I found it, I *made* it, all by myself, the most fun and the deepest thrill. And even now I look back on it the way elderly athletes recall themselves in their prime, the pure joy of every move, every muscle.

Nita, a co-ed at Modesto Junior College, served at Presidential dinner parties. One night, washing dishes in our kitchen, Nita talked with me about her speech contest days back in Turlock. She always liked "Dramatic Interp," and she remembered a boy who had done a reading about "The Legend of Johnny Appleseed." She didn't know where he got the script, but she knew where I could find the boy: Val was a drama major at the College of Pacific in Stockton. I wrote to him; he answered from Pacific's Playhouse up in Calaveras County, and one Saturday morning I drove up in the Caddy with the big tape-recorder in the trunk. When I arrived Val was awake but still in bed, smoking: tall and skinny and handsome with long black hair that came down over the collar of his pajama shirt. He was practicing his lines for the lead in *Harvey*. His studio-bedroom was so bizarre, so wonderfully bohemian—*Playboys* and wine bottles and shirts and socks and shiny Spanish costumes scattered everywhere.

He sat on the edge of his bed with my microphone

in his hand, sat there with his pajama shirt open, and tried to remember how it went, "The Legend of Johnny Appleseed."

The story of John Chapman, he said, "begins up in a little town they called Vermont." I loved that, it gave me goose-pimples to think all the way back to when Vermont was just a *town*.

> Folks never did rightly know John's last name,
> So they figured they'd call him after his trade—
> And that's why they called him
> Johnny Appleseed.

Val paused, looked at the mike, and couldn't remember. I told him it didn't need to be perfect or anything. I gazed at the open *Playboy* on the sill: there was a color picture of a naked girl sitting on a chair holding up a candle, and you could see her nipples. I thought the publisher could be put in jail for that.

Val had it again: "Now John figured that God put him on earth to do just two things: one was to plant apple trees and the other was to read his Bible to people. Most any day you could see him out in his orchard, pickin' his apples and dumpin' 'em in his cellar; you could hear him singin':

> Oh, the Lord is good to me,
> And so I thank the Lord
> For givin' me the things I need,
> The sun, the rain, and the appleseed.
> The Lord is good to me.

Val moved the mike away from him a little as he sang a vigorous baritone. I sat by the revolving spools of tape while he went on in his pajamas. Perfect. Just perfect. I had struck gold in Calaveras County.

Val did little snatches of owls and rabbits and cougars and bears, all the animals hiding in the forest and watching this man, this strange man, all alone, singing and working. The animals talked it over, wonderingly, among themselves. Up a tree, a pair of owls: "Hoo—hoo whoo's that man out there? 'Twoot, 'twoot —he'll kill us all, beware, beware! What do you think, friend hare?"

Friend hare was a frightened little thing and said, "I'm afraid, I surely be," and the cougar stepped in, all mouth and muscle: "I'm not scared, not me." And a dumb bear said, "Me neither."

We followed Johnny Appleseed across the plains, saw him at a settler's cabin and with the Indians, with more voices from the crossing of the continent. At the end, Johnny has grown very old, and he's dozing under a tree, reading his verses. A golden light comes down from the sky—much, much softer this time—John's Guardeen Angel has come back.

The Angel said, "Come on, John, you've got one long last trip to take."

Ever faithful, ever true, Johnny Appleseed is ready. A golden staircase comes down from the sky, and they walk up to heaven together, a little man and an Angel clad in buckskin. "Now would you agree with me that he was the mightiest man you ever did see?"

I was pissing my pants it was so beautiful.

Val flopped back into his messy bed and sighed. "It went something like that."

I had to make a lot of changes. I debated for a long time over single words, over a step, over a rocking of the body in transition. Generally I didn't like all the "a's" in front of words—it was too hayseedy. I tried to give my story-teller dignity, with just a suggestion of "the common" in his voice. And I had to suggest the great Western plains by some vastness in my eyes, a vague spaciousness in a moving palm.

And what Val had given me wasn't *funny* enough. I finally decided I'd speak in my own voice only once, at the very beginning, straight from the shoulder, an announcement simple and clear and restrained: "From *The Treasury of American Folklore*, 'The Legend of Johnny Appleseed.'" From there on I was all sorts of voices, all of them strung together by a wise narrator who could find the humor in life's small moments. When the forest animals were watching Johnny at his planting I really let the cougar rip: he was Cerkoni pantsing me in the rain, the schoolyard bully we all knew, I swung my arm, knocking my sportcoat open, my chin out, all swagger: "I ain't afraid, not me!" And the big old bear was the dumb, reliable captain of the football team: I didn't just say "Me neither,"—I made it into a husky "My nyther," with my massive paws just hanging—those two feeble-minded, lovable words gave folks a moment to guffaw.

My owl-hoot was a happy accident. I found that if I sped up a gurgle, popped it up an octave, loosened my cheeks for a flutter chamber, I could do an exact imitation of an owl. No "hoot-hoot" crap. A real owl in a real forest. It was an astonishing little sound, scary and lonely and true. It made people sit up.

On the tape recorder Val had concluded with that question to the audience:

> Now would you agree with me that he
> Was the mightiest man you ever did see?

And I tried, but I couldn't get it right. The pauses were all screwed up with those internal rhymes:

> Now would you agree
> With me
> That he...

And I had to pause for "mightiest," but then "man you ever did see" never seemed to go just where I wanted it. I did it a dozen different ways and hated to throw it out, but I finally decided to quit at the high point—the golden staircase coming down from the sky and the two of them climbing it together. I tried to get the sense of "mightiest" just in the pause itself and the low-key whisper of

> "a little man"

before opening it up with the true greatness and wise humor of "an angel clad in buckskin," biting down on those hard central consonants, "bu*ck*/*sk*in," holding it right there, then dropping away into myself, my body saying to the audience: you take it, it's yours, it *belongs* to you.

72

Johnny Appleseed couldn't be cute. If I were Mister Pretty Speaker Boy it would all go to ashes. I needed authority and reticence. It had to be a *feeling*, not an "act."

I spent afternoons in apple orchards, climbing in trees. I talked with Ag students majoring in pomology. I went on a hayride. I ate an apple every night after *The Tonight Show*. On the tape Val did Johnny as a baritone, and it seemed wrong to me. I had to do a lot of work on Johnny's singing voice, and finally I found an eerie counter-tenor way up there almost behind my throat, a hollow melody full of yearning.

A new English teacher at Modesto high gave me pause. The first time I'd really noticed Mr. Renner was when he made a guest faculty appearance at a Mu Eta Sigma Assembly at Christmas—some of the guys had been working on a jazz band, and then all of a sudden the big red curtains parted and there were the guys on the drums and sax and bass, with little Mr. Renner standing in front with a silver cornet. A few phrases into it I saw how good he was and I remembered my first appearance on that stage when I did my George Gobel imitation, when I pretended to be as small and forlorn as Mr. Renner looked. The group did "Tenderly," and Mr. Renner was the featured soloist; when he got to the part where the words go

> your arms opened wide
> and closed me inside

he went all the way up into it, so gently, and took it even

higher, a strong little slide that was almost painful—

and closed me *in* - zeeeeee - *side*—

and then cascades of skat notes coming down, glistening, silver. It was so perfect that when it was over everybody just waited a moment. And then the kids were clapping and whistling and stamping their feet, going wild. Mr. Renner wasn't frail or small at all; he was a sliver of steel. He stood there, not bowing or anything, just stood there while the red curtains closed.

Mr. Renner's classroom was right next to the Speech classroom. One day after school I was practicing, and Renner wandered in, said, "Don't stop," and plopping himself down, smoking a Camel, he listened to me doing Johnny A. He tapped his ashes, and nodded his jet black hair absently. When he looked up at me with his steely eyes, I stared back at him through his cigarette smoke. I finished. I said, "Well?"

"You better re-think that Guardian Angel."

Excuse me?

He said the Guardian Angel oughtta sound like Ev Dirksen on the marigold.[1]

What?

He said the Guardian Angel's voice was too close to the voice of Johnny-as-an-Old-Man. He said, "Look, Dan'l, you have to *unleash* Johnny Applesauce— let him range up and down the land. Feed America her fake values!"

Hey, wait a minute, this isn't fake, this is mine. I

---

[1] Everett Dirksen, U.S. Senator 1950-1969; known for his melodramatic, resonant voice, and his wish to have the marigold named the national flower

stared at him.

Sprawled, smoking, he said, "What you gotta do, Dan'l, is give 'em their damn MYTH!" Renner popped his cigarette butt over against a metal filing cabinet and winked at me.

I didn't much like his tone, but I changed the Guardian Angel. And it was better. I could see it in people's faces, I could feel the way they were a little surprised that I could do Pompous America, and they relaxed and settled down ready to listen to the real thing. Good ol' Mr. Renner.

I knew I had Johnny Appleseed right when I was doing it one night out at a Grange pot-luck supper, a grizzled old farmer off at the end of the front table got tears in his eyes. He was embarrassed to be so touched. His wife looked at him, and he smiled sheepishly, turned away from her, crossing his legs, his eyes examining the rafters.

Yes. *Yes!*

It was "The 'Fifties.'" "Optimism For Courageous Living" was June, 1952, on the eve of Eisenhower's election to the Presidency. "Johnny Appleseed" was September, 1956, on the edge of Eisenhower's second term. It was a great time to be an American. We had destroyed Hitler's Germany and Imperial Japan, we had made the world safe for democracy again. We were pure. Johnny Appleseed was religion. How seriously did I believe in God and Country? Johnny Appleseed seriously. This was the one time in all my Speech Contest Career when I really believed in what I was saying. I *loved* it. Were "The 'Fifties" sentimental?—of *course*. So was I. I was 16, for Chrissakes.

From the very beginning I saw the job as getting the audience to laugh at it and love it at the same time. It was all *mine*, Mom and Pop didn't coach me on this one. They stood back and gave me room to play with it. They saw what I was doing. Johnny Appleseed lets you have it both ways—you never quite know what's coming next. Is this kid serious? No. Or—or *is* he? You don't really believe this pastoral baloney, and of course you do, we all do, one way or another. It's not red white & blue bullshit, it's a *dream*, you judge it by how beautiful it is, it's a myth, it's humor, it's a *song*. The thing I enjoyed the most was watching it catch the audience from behind. Sooner or later in all the fun their eyes would change, they'd *get* it. No other country on the face of the earth could have dreamed Johnny up. Wouldn't it be somethin' else if this crazy devil country was as good as we tell ourselves we are? What if we were faithful to our first dream, what if that little dumbfuck is *us*?

I had an act for audiences from 50 to over a thousand. "Johnny Appleseed" wasn't for an Oratory Contest. It was just a thing to make people happy, to make them think, to make them proud.

I stood in a large Baptist Church with a long sanctuary, walls of whitest white and big stained-glass windows depicting events in the life of our Lord. About 500 people had jammed in. Organ music (beloved hymns) and the blessed air-conditioner were going full blast. I walked slowly up past the baptismal fount and ascended the green carpet of the altar. I looked out at the sea of faces. The hope of America is assembled here. Folks, I want to tell you a lovely little story you can believe in. Come in here with me. It won't bite you. Come in here with Johnny—Johnny Appleseed.

When I leaned forward a little, dislocating my glottis and releasing the frightened owl in the forest, it began to kindle, it took off, I could see their faces change. It wasn't a "reading" anymore; it was a past, our past, and I could give it to them only if I could lose myself completely. I got to the moment when Johnny comes upon

> a settler's cabin, blazin' fire
> with a hundred hostile injuns dancing around,
> singin' their song of hate.

My voice began to throb like signal drums:

> Johnny—he never stopped, he walked right
> into the midst of the heathens, pulled out the
> Good Book, and began to read.

I cranked it all the way down, down to Johnny who was terribly scared and terribly brave, his croaky tenor adrift in catastrophe,

> "Thou shalt not kill"

and turned into a hero not because he had any ambitions along that line but just because he was stuck with it— you got to understand he was scared to death and he didn't blink an eye:

"Thou shalt love thy neighbor—as thyself."

My eyes went to the sunlight bursting through the windows, cascading on the whitest, whitest walls, sunlight streaming through the life of Jesus, gentle Jesus meek and mild.

And at the end when Johnny Appleseed was old, and the Guardeen Angel was calling him back to the Great Beyond, I was an old, old man—my voice cracked like a moment of doubt at the end of a great effort: my life, my project, oh, Angel, don't take away from me what I've given all my years to, don't rob me of what I believe in—if you rob me of that you rob me of my life, for my life is what I believe in—

Be honest in your life for once, Danny Boy.

I sat down. I hadn't ever sat down before. Suddenly I seem to be so frail. Danny, you can't *sit down*, not on the green-carpeted steps. But I did. In the Baptist Church where couples are wed, where babies are christened, where caskets are displayed. You gotta get up. Get up!

I sat there.

My whole body hurt.

I had a little spasm in my left eye.

Oh, 500 people are one person, and that thing in my left eye snaps like a loose electric wire. I could feel the audience, feel them rising in the back row, straining for a benediction:

I don't know what i am doing, i am sitting here, it is surely wrong to end sitting down, and i am a fool, i have spent my whole life on a fool's errand, i don't want to, i just don't want to anymore,

but i want it so much, i'll give anything,

*got to get real
real quiet.*

> and they walked up
> to heaven together —
> a little man and an Angel —
> clad in bu<u>ck</u>-<u>sk</u>in

but suddenly it wasn't enough, it wasn't quite there, and those difficult rhymes were coming out in a whisper,

> now wouldn't you agree
> with me
> that he

and the electric wire snapped in my left eye, and oh for goodness sake, a little droplet came out and wandered down my left cheek—I didn't wipe it away, it stopped by itself, above my mouth, and no, no, no, that's way too sentimental—but I'm not blubbering or anything, I'm not weeping, I'm in perfect control, it's only one little tiny drop (or would they think I'd practiced, and learned how to do it, a magic trick, *one* tear?) and then Johnny Appleseed caught *me* from behind, I was whispering—I'd never whispered before, it was the softest, strangest sound, a voice I'd never heard me make before—and I finally understand, I understand at last, in a perfect swoon—

> "…the mightiest man you ever did see."

In the utter silence, the absolute silence of the

church, I sat there. Goodbye, Mr. Fancy. I pulled myself together, stood up to go away.

And then it began. Murmuring and building. I walked slowly up the center aisle of the sanctuary. I could see them now, people—*people my own age*—all the kids were standing to greet me. I didn't care about winning, I just wanted to be loved. By all the friends I never had. And here they were, reaching out. It was a hallucination, vibrating up my legs, spasms crowding in my groin, oh, most bountiful, bracing my torso and filling my chest like warm water. I didn't know what was happening, I was Johnny Appleseed for good, and girls, girls rustling in summer dresses, one with tears of love streaming from her eyes and down her cheeks, coming to me, and a guy, a tall farm boy, solemn as hell, putting his big hand on my shoulder, and I and they—we— oh I made my way, dazed and surrounded, up that aisle, I was a tuning fork for their deepest note —

It was a moment from which I have never recovered.

CHAPTER SIX

CYRANO

"I really did say to myself that I must escape altogether from the impulse to over-achieve."
— Richard Wilbur

"The most powerful magic, working in all these sacraments, is the close presence of other human beings, without competition or one-upping. The original sin is to be on an ego trip that isolates."
— Paul Goodman

"I'm so lonesome I could cry."
— Hank Williams

April 1957, Modesto

By the Spring of my Senior Year at MHS, I was coming to "the climax of a career launched at age twelve," said the Modesto *Bee*. For some time the *Bee* had been saying "DANNY DOES IT" or "McCALL PLACES FIRST" and they called me a MODESTO LAD, YOUTH, BOY who WINS, TRIUMPHS, and WINS AGAIN. Once I was KING OF ORATORY. Frequently they would recapitulate: Louisville, Television Diablo, Lion's, Muscogee, Native Sons of the Golden West. From Oregon, "EX-EUGENIAN WINS" and from Redlands "HOOPER'S GRANDSON CHAMPION" and from close-by, "FORMER STOCKTON BOY SPEECH CHAMP." In the *Bee*, April 22, 1957, my photograph was captioned, "ANOTHER TROPHY," with the story,

> "Guess who won another speech contest?
> Dan McCall, Modesto High School senior who has racked up enough scholarship prizes by speaking in the past year to put him in a higher income tax bracket, did it again last night.
> The prize was—ho-hum—another scholarship."

My only life was the contests and the platforms, and I never questioned what I would do without them.

When I was riding my uni and telling my jokes at a dance intermission, emceeing a program where girls my own age were around, I liked to walk inconspicuously among them for half-an-hour before my number. I was not noticed as anything special, and learned to cultivate that. After, I could bask in the warm, awed stares. I began to try to be worse than inconspicuous, a little shabby and foolish, to walk on the fringes of the dance floor with a limp, ask a girl to dance and hope she would refuse me—so that after the show, after my triumph, the girl would kick herself. It was a delight to fumble before the show, fumble to a girl and know in my heart, say to her without speaking: You will hate yourself in a little while. In the movie *A Face in the Crowd*, Andy Griffith plays a guy who got to be a national TV star and had America in the palm of his hand. Then while the credits were flipping over the image, and the sound on stage was cut off over the music over-lay, he liked to peer into the camera and say, "You poor fools, how you love me, how you stupid people love me." Patricia Neal in the control room suddenly flipped the dials so that he was "on," and America heard, heard everything about how his magic was just a way of playing with them, tricking their hearts. He was dead then.

You have to be careful.

At the University of San Francisco, I entered three events in the District Finals. Original Oratory was the first day, and I wasn't too sure about my speech, "The Tragedy of Jean-Pierre." At the end of my speech I brought it all together in a blasphemy on the 23rd Psalm:

> Science is my shepherd, I shall not want…
> Though I walk through the valley of six lane
>   highways…

> Thy experiments and thy government-financed
> programs, they comfort me…
> And I shall dwell in an air-conditioned nightmare
> forever.

I worried it was too dangerous, somebody might get the wrong impression. Especially at U.S.F. where some of the judges were priests.

But I kept getting "Up's" all day. By the evening there were a dozen of us still in the running. We all knew each other, had heard each other's orations at all the tournaments in the spring. We could recite each other's speeches.

I took the trophy. Next day I made it a clean sweep, with Johnny in Dramatic Interp. and the Priceless Ingredient in Impromptu. When I drove up to the house, two a.m. Sunday morning, I knew I couldn't get all the trophies in—and up—before the folks would hear me. A block from home I stopped and arranged them in the backseat, put the suitcase on the floor. Then I drove into the garage and made a lot of noise and after a few minutes the light came on and Dad was there in his robe—followed in a moment by Mother. "Hi," I said.

Dad wasn't completely awake yet.

"Sorry, didn't mean to wake you."

"How did it go," Mother asked.

"All right. Can you give me a hand with this stuff?"

They walked down into the garage and looked into the back seat. I couldn't get it symmetrical—the three first place trophies were the same as the one from the previous year for *Death of a Salesman*—the standard

"District" cups about two feet high. But with three wins I also walked away with the Sweepstakes, and that was the same design but twice the size. Dad carried it; I carried the two for Original Oratory and Impromptu; Mother, the one for "Johnny Appleseed." Back in my bedroom we tried to see where to put them up, but there wasn't much spare space now, the chest-tops and TV-tops and desktops and nightstands and bookcase were loaded. Mother said, "We need a trophy case."

I flopped on the bed. "It would be more convenient—behind glass, we wouldn't have to dust them as often."

Dad had put the four-footer sweepstakes on the carpet. He stood by it in his robe, his face still creased with sleep, and he heard my casual "won't have to dust them so often," and looked at me, "Oh, you think you're top dog, do you?"

Mother glanced at him and then sat at the foot of my bed.

"*Tell* us about it. Tell us everything."

In my farewell appearance on the stage at Modesto High, one final pep rally, I worked out a skit that Mother and Dad had done at Redlands in the late twenties. Mother stood with her arms clasped behind her right in front of the curtain, Dad behind it; he reached his arms out under her armpits, and while she spoke he did these spooky, awkward gestures—the folks told me it brought down the house. So I worked it out with Darlene, our rally commissioner; she had a splendid sense of humor and plenty of school spirit, and the only problem was that my arms weren't big and hairy. I got a piece of charcoal in the Art Room, and scrawled big black swirls on both forearms, and while she gave her sophisticated speech that I wrote for her, full of polysyllabic nonsense, I was back there with black-chalked arms roaming around and scratching her plastic-reinforced nose and—Mother and Dad never did this: I made a couple of suggestive motions toward her boobs, and she apparently went ARGH! with her face, and the kids went nuts with laughter, they roared and whooped and hollered, and when it was over they thundered their applause as she bowed and bowed.

Then, graciously, she held open the curtain for me to come out, and the applause, you could hear it diminish, partly at the astonishment of seeing me with those chalked-up arms, but mainly the resentment: It's Him Again. I'd been up there too much and we'd already had the Awards assembly where everybody got $300 for Home Ec. at MJC or $150 for Ag. at Davis, but I got $17,000 for Stanford, now they had been taken again by Hot Shot. I ran back behind the curtain where there were clearly audible groans.

I sat in the Caddy under the big trees behind the Speech building. It was almost four o'clock and I held myself rigid behind the wheel, alternately holding my breath for as long as I could and then breathing deeply, making myself dizzy, trying to faint. They groaned—the kids *groaned*.

Mr. Renner came out of the building, saw me doing my breathing, stopped, and looked; I let my head roll back. He had seen me running off the stage after the groans. He stood beside my window. "You okay, Danny?"

"Oh," I said, "when you're Number One, everybody's out to get you."

He silently looked across my hood.

"I don't mean to keep you," I said, and put my head forward on the wheel. After I had done "Johnny Appleseed" for one of his English classes, he had said to me afterward, "Well, I can see how it won"—almost as if it was *bad* to have won.

He waited and then said, "Give me a lift home?"

"OK."

Good 'ol Mr. Renner got in beside me, putting his briefcase on the floor.

"They groaned," I said.

"Who?"

"The kids, at assembly. They loved my idea, they liked the skit, but then they saw me, and they —"

"Yeah, but what do they know."

I looked at him and I couldn't tell who he was making fun of. I drove.

"You can't have it both ways," he said at last.

I was starting to get some confidence back, and I hoped he didn't think I was in need of counseling. "A lot of kids are my friends, you know, like Bonnie and Irvin and —"

"And if you add up their IQ's they almost equal yours."

I just missed the light and we had to sit there in the middle of the crosswalk.

"Friendship isn't charity," he said.

"I know."

"I've watched you. When you run into trouble with people you blot it out and go win another speech contest."

I smiled, watching for the green light. "It's better than the other way."

"What's that?"

"Blot it out and go lose a speech contest."

He smiled at that, and lit a cigarette. We were almost equals, and I appreciated it. But then he said, "Why are you so insecure?"

"Oh, I'm the least insecure kid I know." The light changed, and I popped across the intersection, zipping along ahead of the dumb Chevy on my right.

"The perfect world has room for just one person," he said, scrunching down in the seat.

"I don't want to live in that world. Who'd there be to applaud?"

He sighed. "Dan, you know what you are?"

I waited.

"*Pure.*"

That tickled me, and I kept cool. "Pure what?"

"And you know what you're doing." He flicked the cigarette out the window. "That's the depressing thing, you know exactly what you're doing."

He lit up another cigarette. "But you can't solve a human failure with a trophy." He sagged in the seat. "I'm not sure my solution's any better."

"What's that?"

"Solve one human failure with another one."

I kept quiet for a while after that, and turned where he told me to. A few blocks down McHenry I said, "That's an awful thing to say."

"Well Danny, wait a few years. You'll get the feel of it."

Again I was quiet for a few blocks. I felt vaguely

happy. I pretended he was my coach and I was the star quarterback, senior year, flooded with offers and scouts coming around. A big decision was on the way, and he was givin' it to me straight. Danny, I've taught you everything I know—now you're going far out of little Modesto, to follow your star. Be careful, Danny, and Godspeed.

My image got to me and I suddenly blurted out, "Do you think I should go to a psychiatrist, just for a little while, so maybe I could understand myself?"

"Understanding," he said, "is the easy part."

I was showing off a little with my driving, I somehow felt that he couldn't drive very well, and I zipped up to a stop at the curb in front of his house.

He dropped the cigarette out into the gutter, readying himself to go. "Dan, what are you going to do if you grow up?"

"If?" I said like a fool, and then saw how slow I'd been, and was embarrassed. I'd failed him, after he'd talked to me straight-from-the-shoulder. I muttered something about going to Stanford and then…

"Well," he said, opening the door, "just so long as you don't become another Richard Nixon."

He smiled at me, bending with the door open.

"Hey, can we have another talk sometime—coach?"

"Anytime," he said. "Keep your zipper up." He shut the door, and I drove on, watching him hold his hand up to me through my rear view mirror.

Later that night I stood under a streetlamp outside my parents' house, in my father's red silk robe, scrawling words down on a piece of paper. I was writing my autobiographical poem for graduation. I'd heard that jazz poetry was the big thing in the coffee houses up in San Francisco, so I let her rip. I knew how to sling words around, I'd only been waiting my whole life to tear the roof off. I realized I'd have to say disagreeable things, play with the darker emotions. The poem frightened me, it suddenly sprung up on me, and I had to walk outside, walk the words growling out of me:

> Break, oh break the windows, unscrew the doors
> from my jams, Suicide! Break
> *all* the windows,
> O Captain, My Captain this trip is almost
>
> done, and I have too long
> thrown myself out of high places
> where I so richly live, O
>
> man, I'm in a white MG with the door
> open at 110 mph
> not in the least intending to jump
>
> I'm not your American Champ,
> not Boy of the Year,
> can't you see how tired I am
> of being
> Danny Boy, A Kid
> With a Sore Throat —
>
> My unicycle grows under me,
> I lift my feet onto the pedals and ride, ride
> all over the universe, way up
> into outer space, a swoon into soft dark

>everything,
>   not in the least intending to
>   (JUMP, roars the big bassoon)

The next morning I submitted it to *Sycamore Leaves*, the Modesto High School Literary Magazine, and the editors said they'd publish it. It was scheduled to come out on the last day of school. That pleased me, it would let everybody know. Finally.

But when the magazine came out, my poem wasn't included. I decided it was better that way.

The previous summer, in 1956, I had enrolled in the Northwestern University School of Speech and Drama, the "Cherub" program for gifted students. It was a six-week deal—two hundred of us, half in Forensics and half in Theatre Arts.

On to Northwestern by rail: a milk-train, sweaty and dirty, jerking to unscheduled stops, waiting on the central plain at three a.m., full of defunct high school debaters hot and miserable, sleepless in grubby frustration, holding on until Evanston. On campus, a vague, humid exuberance of "theatre" hung over dorm life.

We had to make the rounds of the directors, trying out for the parts. Howard, the director of *Cyrano de Bergerac*, was a chunky little man with delicate fingers, hopelessly near-sighted, and after the reading I talked with him for a long time. He held me and kept me with him while the others went on to the next one. He asked me to say, "I too have loved" as if I had never said it before. He pretended to be Cyrano's friend, and as he strolled away from me he looked me straight in the eye, "Now," he said —

I was determined to have good eye contact. But then maybe I wasn't supposed to. It was a classroom. I held myself, softly, whispering, "I too have loved."

Howard said, "Now do it completely different." He walked away, ready with his question, and I watched his chunky form in casual attire, and before he even got to his cue I blurted, helpless rage and self-doubt: "I too have loved."

He smiled.

"I did it right?"

"No." Howard sat on the chair-arm. He was looking for something in me. "No, you mustn't do it like that at all."

Think of Cyrano's grotesque nose—*you are ugly*—

Think of what you most regret, Danny. Some love hopelessly lost.

I can't. I looked into his four eyes.

Danny, have you ever slept with a woman?

Well....

Danny, tell the truth—tell it by saying "I too have loved."

"I—too—I have loved—"

He touched me. "I'll teach you," he said, "how to do it." His delicate fingers explored his knees.

When the cast lists were posted, there I was—Cyrano: Dan E. McCall. Our director had seen Jose Ferrer do *Cyrano* on Broadway, and he taught me all sorts of special tricks that he'd learned from that production. Howard was an absolute fanatic about sword fighting and got a guy on the Northwestern fencing team to coach me. I bought my own epee. My partner and I practiced two hours a day on the grassy lawn in front of the dorm or out on the little beach of Lake Michigan. We got really good; I could slip my blade under his and spin his sword right out of his hand high up into the air and catch it, cracking poetry.

A lot of the classes were boring. I decided they were for the kids who didn't have big parts, just to keep them busy. Scene Design was dumb carpentry work, Make-Up and History of Costume were silly. So I cut my classes and spent my afternoons at Wrigley Field, pullin' for the Cubs and Ernie Banks. Nights I'd go to jazz spots like Mr. Kelly's when I could get someone over 21 from Northwestern to sneak me in.

Cyrano was shaping up. At dress rehearsal they trained a spot on me from down in the pit, and it threw a huge grotesque shadow of my profile up against the cyclorama, my ghastly putty nose. Thank God we ran through it in full make-up. In dress rehearsal I kissed Roxanne's hand, my nose banged against her wrist, got loosened and fell off during the sword fight.

So there I was on opening night: ready for the poignant agony of Cyrano de Bergerac. Our swordplay drew a few outbursts of spontaneous applause, and my nose didn't fall off. After the "I too have loved" scene, a flower-girl said to me in an embarrassed whisper, "You were good tonight." I tried to capture the intonations and rhythms of a despondent suitor, a disfigured lover with a passionate heart and a rambunctious brain.

The performance was fine enough; a full house, a couple cries of "Bravo." At the cast party Howard told me that several people had come around to tell him it was the finest fencing, amateur or professional, they had ever seen on stage. That helped a little, but I felt strangely subdued and let down.

That night I couldn't sleep, I lay awake for a long time. Then I heard scratching on my door. I pulled myself out of bed to find Howard at the entry, making "come here" motions. I put on my robe and walked outside with him along the shore of the lake. He was a little drunk, I could see that. He kept muttering "dedication." By a pier he stopped. "The faculty of the Cherub program had their meeting tonight, to vote for the awards: one boy and one girl from Forensics, one boy and one girl from Theatre Arts."

The best four would get scholarships to Northwestern. I was the lead in the biggest play; if I didn't get it, I would have failed in my responsibility.

I smiled at Howard, his boozy confusion, his four-eyes. "And?"

"You didn't get one."

I ran down to the lake and waded in up to my knees, soaking the hem of my robe.

"Danny—Danny —"

"Well, Goddamn it, *why?*"

"Because"—he staggered a bit and reached out and joined me in the lake in the moonlight, he didn't take his shoes off—"we all thought you were brilliant, we all said yours was the best acting performance of the summer. But some staff thought you loved yourself more than the theatre." He fell back a little, almost sat down in the water, and grabbed my shoulder for support. "The Costume Mistress was especially displeased by your lack of interest and cooperation. She said you rarely came to class, and didn't help clean up."

"What *is* this!" I snarled at him in the moonlight. You're supposed to choose the *best*! Not the *nicest*.

I kicked the water. "To hell with them. They're out to get me—all summer they've been out to get me."

"No, Danny." He looked at the moon and he looked at me.

I stomped back in my soggy robe through the water, "Fuck it."

Danny," he turned, "don't prove them right."

"How," I shouted, "can I prove them *wrong*?"

Sitting around for two days watching all the kids pack up and go home, I thought about it, slowly turning it over and over in my imagination. I tried to tell myself that this one didn't count: who cares about a tuition scholarship to Northwestern? Be serious man, you are going to *Stanford*!

But God, it hurt. I had the Number One talent but I lacked the character. I failed to show the common courtesy, I didn't have the basic human decency. Yes, indeed, Danny Boy is an outstanding thespian, but underneath it all… well…

On the long train ride back across America, all the way from Chicago to San Francisco, for two days and two whole nights, sitting up, I slept fitfully and had terrible nightmares. The morning of the second day the soldier traveling beside me said I cried in my sleep. He said the talky old woman sitting behind us had leaned forward and patted my shoulder for several miles. He laughed and said the woman sang me a lullaby. I thought of telling him I was a heroin addict experiencing withdrawal. Instead I went and stood outside in the fresh air between the swaying cars. Where nobody could hear, I began screaming at the beautiful dumb landscape lurching by—amber waves of bullshit!

CHAPTER SEVEN

PROUD PATRIOTS AND ENLIGHTENED CITIZENS

"To be a talker, to be 'eloquent,' was to be American."
— Ann Douglas

"I grew out of it, and I'm now very critical of it, but I lived it. So now I make films about it. The bad value of it, the false value: putting all the emphasis on winning. And there's no greater example of it than America. There are two high points in American life: money and winning. It's so instilled in American Life."
— Robert Redford

"Winning isn't everything: it's the only thing."
— Vince Lombardi

1957, Waterville, Maine

The hardest—the *hardest*—was the last one. In the American Legion High School Oratory Contest of 1957, you had to give a ten-to-twelve minute prepared oration and then a four-to-six minute extemporaneous speech on any one of twelve paragraphs of the Constitution, the paragraph picked by chance at each contest. At the National Finals, I had no fear of the Florida boy (he lacked the killer instinct and wanted to go into the ministry), but the Michigan boy and the New York boy were like me: battle-hardened veterans of the forensic wars, we were the last guys standing, the blood of the vanquished all over us.

Waterville seemed like an odd place for a National Finals, but in the twenty years of the contest, the American Legion had never settled the championship in Maine. After I won the Western States round, Mom and I had to fly to Waterville. Modesto Post 74 paid for me; Dad, again for Mother. I'd had a lot of fun, actually, climbing the steps of the ladder: Modesto, Lodi, San Francisco, Salt Lake City. In Salt Lake I'd had a scare and won by only a single point over the kid from Nebraska; after the contest one of the judges, a Judge in real life, told me he gave me third place because I said in my extempore that the Supreme Court Justices had to be faithful to the promises they made on *election* day. He was shocked that I'd made it all the way to the Regional Finals thinking that the Supreme Court was elected.

The contestants were stuck in the bone-numbing

damp of the local Waterville Inn. Mother and I had to sleep in our robes. The creaky old Gothic hotel was crazy, a gabled place with weird little half-flights and wings.

On the front page of the Waterville *Morning Sentinel*, under a photo of the finalists in our bibs with the caption "First Lobster Treat":

> "The four finalists in the American Legion national high school oratorical contest who arrived in Waterville Wednesday have almost been kept in the equivalent of a TV isolation booth. This is done so that the five judges will have no advance information concerning their personal history or record which might even subconsciously color their decision."

I didn't much like the way New York and Michigan did most of their talking with each other, as if Florida and I were no threat. Wouldn't it be something to lose—win and win and win and win and then in your last big one, the National Championship worth $4,000, the one where all the papers would carry it, the one where the winner would be flown to New York to appear on the *Today* show with Dave Garroway, the really big one where God and Country come together to culminate one career and announce the auspicious beginning of a new one—to come in second? Or—or *third*?

I was a little cheered by seeing Terry Ann Poulin, she'd had a few lines in *Cyrano* back at Northwestern; now she was a senior at Waterville High, and in the evening she had a reception for all the finalists and their families in her parents' home on Silver Street. She had invited only the best people. In the middle of the punch and Pat Boone records she asked me if I would do that wonderful reading I had done for our acting class at Evanston. I said of course, and everybody gathered around on the couches and on the floor, but I was especially eager to see how Toth (Michigan) and Everingham (New York) were taking it. At the end everybody applauded, and Mrs. Poulin was especially effusive. By the end, with Johnny old and under the tree, I got into it again and forgot about the other finalists; but the second it was over I was looking at them. I didn't know anymore whether I really believed it or whether it was a con-job. I wasn't sure there was a difference.

The morning of the contest when we had to draw for speaking positions out of a big straw hat, I went first and got position #1. My heart sank—nobody would warm the audience up for me. When Michigan saw the dismay on my face he smiled, "That's your reward for being grabby." I don't know why drawing Speaker #1 upset me so much—I'd been in first speaking position several times, even in the all-or-nothing final round at Muskogee, but in the lobby of that cold little Waterville hotel, when I drew the card out of the gray hat, I was frantic. I ran back up the shabby two flights, down the freezing hall, up the little half-flight, into the cold room where Mother was waiting. I whimpered under the blankets, "It's all over."

Mother tried to help. She asked me what was the matter. I was seventeen now, not twelve, and I didn't wear cute little white shit. "Nothing. But it's no use—

I've lost."

I had not done Johnny Appleseed with a clean heart at the Poulins' house on Silver Street, I had used him as a weapon to frighten Everingham and Toth, and now I was going to pay for it.

The finals were held at an assembly at Waterville High, the auditorium beautified with red-white-and blue bunting, every seat filled and chairs lining the aisles. Nine hundred kids and honored guests from Colby College and dignitaries. The head judge was Governor Edmund Muskie. The four speakers wandered around backstage, warming up.

All of a sudden I was out there, doing it:

> "When Robert Louis Stevenson was a small boy he stood one evening by his window watching the village lamplighter at work. Young Robert cried, 'Oh, look, I can see something wonderful—there's a man coming down our street punching holes in the dark!' In 1787 a group of consecrated men trod the highways of humanity punching holes in the darkness of their day."

I had to stand helplessly backstage and listen to the others. Everingham of New York went next; I knew I was in trouble when I heard the power in his opening sentences:

> "It is early spring of 1775. The shot heard round the world has been fired. The fight

for freedom has begun."

Wow. It was like *You Are There*. He had a steely voice, no fooling around. He played for keeps.

My legs began to go. I had to sit down.

And then it got worse.

Toth, the crew-cut Michigan boy, was a Catholic, and his Coach was a Priest. He had endless kindness and goodness in his voice:

> "It's not enough to be free when we shun the Negro on our buses or in public places because he has a different ancestry or a different colored skin. It's not enough—"

He had a whole list of "It's not enough's —" and he was so impressively dignified. Yes, Toth was on the mountain-top of virtue, calling us to our national commitment.

I went down the empty hall and stood, sick, in the boys' room. I didn't even hear Florida—at best I was third. Oh God, I've lost the big one.

On the plane home from Waterville, Mom'll be right there beside me—maybe she'll sing the lullaby to me like the lady on the train from Chicago when I cried in my sleep. I've blown the whole thing. It's not Water*ville*, it's Water*loo*.

There was a "Musical Interlude" after the prepared orations. The Waterville high school student orchestra squeaked away while the contestants gathered in the science room with the national chairman of the Americanism Program. He was wearing an Army cap.

No way I was going to be *grabby* this time. I let Florida pick the extemp topic.

A lucky break.

"Amendment X."

My spirits soared. Couldn't be better. Powers Not Delegated. Sure. Oh, that's beautiful. I clicked it into place in my mind: "The powers not delegated by the Constitution, nor prohibited by it to the States, are reserved to the States respectively, or to the people." What I'd do is use that stuff I got from listening to the St. Ignatius boy's oration in San Francisco—it thrilled me then, and it would work to perfection now:

> "The Russian Constitution claims that the ultimate power resides in the State. But when ultimate power belongs to the State, that power can be taken away from the people. In our Constitution, in the last section of the Bill of Rights, the power belongs to the people. It belongs to us—and nobody can take it away from us. The genius of our founding fathers was their realization:
>
> Above All, Humanity."

Bingo! I had it now. Oh yes, I got a shot.

I walked on air in the science room. I talked to my hands and went to the window. I talked to the leaden sky and the icy rain. Then I took my place in the wings, just off-stage. The Americanism Director went out and read the topic to the audience, and it was—it was—not X.

No.

XX!

Holy Shit, it's not 10, it's *20*, it's The Lame Duck Amendment. What's the *matter* with me? Now what do I say? I think it has to do with changing the Presidential inauguration from March to January. There's nothing interesting to say about it. The Constitution has to change with the times? Big deal. They needed the extra months back in the 18th century, without railroads or anything. Think of the time it takes for news to get from Virginia to Vermont. They didn't have telephones. This amendment involves particular social circumstances, and the Founding Fathers were setting down basic principles. Or something. Or something!

I didn't even know the Supreme Court wasn't elected. XX isn't prohibition, is it? No, it's the Lame Duck. Three-fourths of the states have to ratify it, right? The will of the people, the consent of the governed, or whatever. I am walking out on the stage now, and I am going to lose this one. I spoke in a dream, I think I even stuck "The Priceless Ingredient" in there somewhere, which didn't make any sense at all—

The audience seemed restless. Those Waterville kids were really trying to be good, but the competition was going on too long, and they didn't want to be cooped up inside on a rainy day with all this patriotic crap. I looked out among them, but I couldn't spot Mother anywhere. I did a little walk—I walked because I didn't have anything to say—"It's flexible, it moves with the times!" Great. Just great

I could barely stand to hear the others. Everingham said something about this being one of the features of the Constitution that we might re-think in our age of high-speed communications, and then Toth said something about while some might amend this early principle, it still provided an essential safety feature. I didn't understand anything except that I had lost.

It was over and the judges were marking their ballots. I wobbled back out the stage door and went into the science room. I clenched my fists in front of my eyes. Oh well, Danny, take it like a man. Nobody says you have to win the last one. Be gracious in defeat.

I stood around hemorrhaging.

New York and Michigan came back into the room looking pleased, they stood together chatting like honorable adversaries. I was just by myself. Maybe I couldn't even beat Florida. That would be a kick—finish your career in *last place*.

I went outside and around to the front of the auditorium and I walked around in the misting rain. A bunch of guys were laughing outside, they just couldn't stand it anymore, all this speech crap. I had no one in the world to turn to.

Except Mother.

I came up a little ramp and sneaked down the aisle to where Mom was sitting. Oh God. "Hi."

She turned among the young people. "Danny." She looked around herself quickly, I wasn't supposed to be there.

Help me—help me—I've lost, Mother —

She smiled as if to say, "You've got it, my Son."

Don't Mother, don't be nice to me now—we've come over 3,000 miles from California to this cold little two-bit town in Maine and now I've lost, I could have been whisked to New York and appeared on National TV, but —

Mother in her lucky hat and her necklace and her earrings and her gloves and her bag—she looked radiant with Mrs. Poulin beside her. Then she blew me a kiss—Mother blew me a kiss!

The Michigan boy's mother looked real cool, but her heart wasn't singing.

Which means—

I nodded one last time to Mother and then slipped up the aisle, down the ramp, and out and around again in the rain through the backstage door.

Finally it was time to announce the winner. The orchestra did another lame little thing, and Governor Muskie had to make it official.

Fourth was Loomis of Florida, just like I figured, and he seemed happy enough. Third was certainly a possibility for me, and then Toth of Michigan was the one. He bravely asked his Priest to stand up in the audience. The Priest did, and the Maine kids clapped for a Priest.

I was waiting for my name in "the runner-up spot," as the announcer's eyes focused directly in on mine when he spoke the name—what a cruel man to do it that way, so cruel of him to make the New York boy think he had it, and that I was second, and then looking at me he said "Theodore Everingham," and the audience let out a whoop—Lord God in Heaven, I couldn't believe it—and I didn't go into my fainting spell because Ted had to come up and accept, and I couldn't see for a few seconds, I hope I don't wake up now, it's all over, I am the champion, I'm through for awhile, the pressure's off, I won't have to sit around and wait for verdicts anymore —

I stepped up to the podium and Governor Muskie gave me my four thousand bucks for Stanford. I looked up at him and he looked down at me, his face a mixture of amusement and satisfaction. While everybody went on applauding, the portly Americanism Director took me aside and said that I wasn't really supposed to know, but the verdict was unanimous: five straight firsts, no question about it.

As the applause thundered down they brought Mom up onto the stage, and she threw out her arms, and we hugged. We had to stand together for the photographers. The applause was still going on while I took the certificate, and in my mind I was calling home to Dad, I didn't want to make the Louisville mistake and let the reporters get to him first, I'd listen to the cross-country stitching of long distance lines, Dad would answer that way he does, "EeeLo," and I'd say, "Good aftarnuune, Doktar Frankenschtein, dis ist der monster kallink," and then I'd drop character and just say, "Well, it worked out again —"

But truly, I don't think I was so hot. Maybe I didn't have to "rise to the occasion" anymore, I just can't lose, I'm a built-in automatic champion. Maybe people can tell it just by looking at my face, my walk, and people can't vote against it. Why do I always put myself through the same dumb agony every time, why do I always convince myself I'm a loser, the same old story, when I'm the opposite same old story, I'm a winner? Why do I always torture myself?

I whispered to Mom, "My extemp was so bad, I didn't *say* anything."

"Oh, Danny," she whispered back, laughing, "None

of you said anything—but you said it first!"

The applause finally settled down and everyone went back to their seats. Okay, I'll say something just for you guys. Hey, I'm just like you. I don't give a shit about the Supreme Court or Amendments to the Constitution, but how do you like Elvis getting drafted into the army?

I did a couple of Elvis jokes. I stepped forward to the front edge of the stage—I'm not an orator, I'm a unicycle rider, a tap-dancer—"Elvis is going to be the first soldier in the United States Army who can stand at attention and go on maneuvers at the same time!" I laid a pelvic thrust on 'em, ka-bam!

They went wild.

I stood there grinning with the big check in my hand, the laughter cascading. I turned back to Muskie who was chuckling.

The laugh awakened me from the spell. They were so relieved after an hour and a half of patriotism and Lame Ducks, all the red white and blue solemnity, that when I threw Elvis at them they were more than grateful, this solemn National Finals Assembly that their parents forced them to attend. I didn't think I should do "Phonetic Punctuation," but somehow it was right for the National Finals of Oratory. So I slimmed it down and did an abbreviated little version just for flavor. It took about three minutes and I could feel Florida and Michigan and New York stuck in the ugly chairs behind me. It was wonderful: you guys don't think I really take this contest business seriously, do you?, I was loose and they were with me, but I didn't put the departing horse's fart in, I substituted a *real* kicker, that brought the kids and the adults back together. "But don't let me be 'frivolous' too long," I said, "for we owe this debt to the Legion and to this day, that certain things really are serious, and true—that there are no easy answers in this world but that complexity is too often a way of avoiding situations that demand simple courage, that we all owe a debt to those who remind us that words like bravery and responsibility are not just for Commencement or the Fourth of July, but qualities of self—I'm very happy right now and want to thank you, all of you…"

As the applause rained down again Edmund Muskie said to me, "Swell acceptance speech. You ought to go into public service."

I turned, startled, and looked up at him: that big tall man with a craggy face like Abraham Lincoln's. He put his arm around my shoulder and smiled down at me, the Governor of the State of Maine.

The next day, in the Waterville *Morning Sentinel*:

CALIFORNIA YOUTH WINS AMERICAN LEGION ORATORICAL CONTEST

A 17-year-old California high school senior was crowned national high school speaking champion here Thursday afternoon in the finals of the annual American Legion oratorical contest. Dan E. McCall of Modesto, Calif., emerged the winner among four finalists in the national contest which was held at Waterville Senior High School and was awarded a $4,000 scholarship. He will enter Stanford University in the fall and expects to major in speech and dramatics and hopes to find his way onto TV or the stage.

Those who heard him Thursday afternoon, especially in his impromptu talk after being awarded first prize, agreed that he has the talent for the field he has chosen. McCall's mother, Mrs. Roy C. McCall, was in Waterville to see him win the coveted honor and was overjoyed at his victory. His father, Dr. McCall, is president of Modesto Junior College.

Within an hour after the contest closed McCall was aboard a plane at LaFleur Airport in Waterville and on his way to New York City where he will make a guest appearance this morning on the Dave Garroway TV show, *Today*. He will also appear on the *Strike It Rich* program.

In winning his way to the top spot in the contest which nation-wide saw 350,000 high school participants, the tall good-looking McCall had to place first in eight different contests beginning with competition in the Modesto High School several weeks ago.

McCall changed the serious tempo of the afternoon's program to a light note briefly in an impromptu talk accepting the first prize. Such a contest proves, he said, that "teenagers aren't just interested in Elvis Presley." But he hastened to add, with a smile, that he "doesn't have anything against Elvis, who is a good clean American boy doing in public what others do in private."

DAN MCCALL DELIVER=
CONGRATULATIONS ON WINNING
THE AMERICAN LEGION 1957
ORATORICAL CONTEST. I AM SURE
EACH OF THE OUTSTANDING
FINALISTS GAVE YOU A REAL
BATTLE FOR THE TITLE YOU
WON. I WAS PRIVILEGED TO WIN
THE 1941 CONTEST AND I KNOW
FROM PERSONAL EXPERIENCE
THAT EVERY CONTESTANT IN
THIS PATRIOTIC PROGRAM IS A
WINNER. BY PARTICIPATING YOU
AND YOUR FELLOW CONTESTANTS
THROUGHOUT THE NATION
HAVE PREPARED YOURSELF TO
BECOME BETTER AMERICANS.
YOU HAVE ACQUIRED AN
UNDERSTANDING AND DEVOTION
TO THOSE PRINCIPLES EXPRESSED
IN THE CONSTITUTION THAT
ARE THE SAFEGUARD OF OUR
DEMOCRATIC GOVERNMENT: THE
BLUEPRINT FOR INTELLIGENT
AMERICAN CITIZENSHIP AND
THE MOTIVATION FOR MEN AND
NATIONS STILL STRIVING TO BE
FREE. AGAIN MAY I EXTEND MY

SINCERE CONGRATULATIONS ON THIS COVETED VICTORY. THE LEGION PROGRAM SPONSORS THE ORATORICAL CON TEST TO ENSURE THAT TODAY'S YOUTH WILL BE TOMORROW'S PROUD PATRIOTS AND ENLIGHTENED CITIZENS.

—FRANK CHURCH, UNITED STATES SENATOR

CHAPTER EIGHT

STRIKE IT RICH

"Autobiography is only to be trusted when it reveals something disgraceful. A man who gives a good account of himself is probably lying."
— George Orwell

"All of us have done things in our lives we'd rather not have done, things that flood us with remorse or pain or embarrassment whenever we call them to mind. If we could erase them from our memories, would we? Should we? Aren't our memories, both the good and the bad, the things that make us who we are? Is a pain-free set of memories an impoverished one?"
— Robin Marantz Henig,
"The Quest to Forget"

"You've got to be honest; if you can fake that, you've got it made."
— George Burns

1957, New York City

When Mother and I got to NBC studios for the *Today* show, the National Commander of the American Legion was there on his artificial legs. I chatted with Emmett Kelley, the greatest clown of them all, who showed me his little broom. I said I was pleased to meet him, and he said, "Likewise I'm sure." The National Commander clicked to attention on his steel pins and warned me that I'd have to take the microphone with authority, really show my stuff, or they'd cut me off. I worked out quickly the best parts of my Legion Oration, and decided on the Optimism speech. Finally the Battle of Attu and Harry Emerson Fosdick's fidelity to his future wife were going to make it coast to coast. Dave Garroway chatted with me on camera, and then I did couple of minutes from my oration; but I was already looking ahead to our next stop on *Strike It Rich*, I'd been told that that show was taped, and it would be re-broadcast out in California the following week. Maybe we could have a little party in my trophy room in Modesto, when we could all watch the re-run. A real party. But who could I invite?

They took us in a limousine to CBS Studios and the *Strike It Rich* set. The Commander was saying I had done a "first-rate job" on *Today*. Gray-haired women were lined up to be in the studio audience, talking along the sidewalk. The Commander motioned to us, "We'll go in this way."

Mother and I slowly walked with him through the shade of the brownstone to the sunless steps of the stage door. Inside, high, taut ropes stood in a line, like prison bars, on one brick wall. Beyond, on the stage proper, a small cardboard-looking set. In front of it stood three cameras. We stepped over the spider-webbing of cords on the floor. A voice from nowhere called, "Let 'em in!" and two guys about my age in CBS uniforms went briskly up the aisles. Shortly, the thin gray line of parcel-burdened women was coming into the darkened rows of theatre sets. The women sat pointing at the stage and whispering to each other.

A handsome man in short sleeves came out to the stage. He called out to a technician, "Did you get the other one?" He stopped short, and blocking the glare with his arm, looked out to the audience. "Oh pardon me, I didn't know we had company. Ladies, I'll be talking with you soon. For now just make yourselves comfortable—and when Warren gets here, don't sit on your hands."

The women giggled. They were happy.

The stage manager's arm came down on my shoulder. "You come with me."

I walked behind him to the metal stairs winding up to the dressing rooms. He motioned for me to have a seat in one of the little rooms. "All right Dan, the contestant today is named Edna Murray. She and her husband own a farm, but the husband had a back injury, can't work, and now they're in danger of losing everything. If you can help her answer the questions correctly, we'll pay off the Murrays' debt and get them back on their feet. Got it?"

"Yep."

The stage manager looked at me and smiled. "There

might be a surprise in this for you too, Danny."

A Corvette? I'll bet it's a Corvette.

He turned to leave. "You wait right here, the director will be in soon."

I sat and looked at myself in the lighted mirror. I felt lonely. I winked at my image and waited and winked again. I thought I saw a pimple on my temple.

I was just going after that pimple when the dressing room door opened and a man smoking a briar pipe came in. His first word was said wonderfully, his mouth full of a melted Hershey bar. "Hi."

"Hi."

"I'm Frank, and you're Dan."

We shook hands.

We grinned at each other and had a fake understanding. Hello, how are you?— Let me be the first to shake you by the throat.

Frank was successful, beardless and masculine and cologned; when he corrected the hang of his coat he twitched sharply as if a bolt of electricity had just been shot through his spine. His hand shook. A drinker. He opened a large black book, and each page was encased in plastic covers, like a specimen, Exhibit A.

"Now these are questions that I'm sure an Americanism Orator could answer, but we're afraid that the light and tension, you know, of being on coast-to-coast television could make you tighten up and forget the answers that in normal circumstances you would just remember right off the bat." His eyes were down, moving, reading something a long time ago. Selling Used Thunderbirds. "So we're going to go over them a little here first. And you don't need to tell anyone about it. Just remember, these are questions you would know, ordinarily, and we want to rehearse them with you so you won't forget."

"OK."

He took the shining book up onto his lap and leafed through it. "Now let me see here. We'll give you some fairly hard ones, an Americanism Champ"—he savored that, "an Americanism Champ." Looking through the plastic pages, at last he raised his eyes: "Here's one— what is the same word for something you ride in and someone who trains athletic teams?"

I knew the answer was easy, but the situation blacked out my mind.

Frank let the book drop so that the plastic glittered a moment, reflecting the mirror light, and a red line was under the answer to my eyes looking at the upside down printing. He pulled on his empty polished pipe and repeated, "One word which means both something you ride in and someone who trains teams, football teams."

I looked in the mirror and seeing my lips moving I turned my eyes back to the print at the man's crotch, and read: "That would be—I guess—'Coach.'"

He looked at my face. We locked eyes. He said, "You catch on."

I shrugged.

We just sat there.

"What's the capital of Brazil?"

"Rio de Janeiro, I think. Or Buenos Aires." [2]

It's Rio. Now remember that. Rio. Rio, red. Got it?"

"Rio, Red." I tried to be ironic. How could they get away with it every day, coast-to-coast?

---

[2] Three years later, in 1960, the capitol was changed to Brasilia.

Frank sighed morosely. "Let's see, we've got to get two more. Could you name three songs by George Gershwin?"

"Oh, that's easy. 'Someone to Watch Over Me,' 'Rhapsody in Blue,' 'An American in Paris,' 'Concerto in F'—"

"Three's enough." He flickered. "And don't say them so fast. You know, hunt around for them. Like they say at Kodak, 'Got the picture'?"

I didn't say anything.

"We got to get you a biggie. Here it is. Who was the first woman doctor in America?"

I smiled. "That *is* a biggie."

Come on, Americanism Champ, the first woman doctor?"

"Couldn't you ask me something about the Constitution? It would fit in with the award."

He let it go. "Elizabeth Blackwell. Got that? E-liz-a-beth Black-well. Can you remember?"

"Yes."

"Say it."

"E-liz-a-beth Black-well."

"Not like that. I was just making sure —"

"I know."

Frank rose from his chair and extended his right hand to me, opening the door with his left. "Okay, Champ. We're glad to have you aboard *Strike It Rich*. And you'll be glad too. There'll be a big surprise in it for you."

People keep saying that. A Corvette. I know it's a Corvette. "And all I have to do is answer the questions?"

"That's right."

"Will there be any other questions?"

"No—it's all—no, you just go on back and sit with your people until Lee comes out for the warm-up. Then come on backstage and wait for him to call you. You won't meet Warren until you go on—got to keep this honest and unrehearsed, you know." He puffed his empty pipe.

"Thanks for the help."

"Anytime, Champ, anytime."

I smiled like William Holden going into the Stalag 17 tunnel. If we should meet again, let's just forget we ever knew each other.

Frank stayed at the door, reading my eyes. He didn't like me at all.

I went back down the metal stairs and rejoined Mother and the Commander. They asked me what news I had. I said the director just explained the rules. Mother wondered if I got any idea of what kind of questions I could expect. I looked at the Commander, and wondered just how much he knew. Behind us housewives were listening, they'd seen me come down the stage-stairs. "It'll go all right," I said quietly to everybody.

The lights cast high roped shadows in the gray dusty wings of the *Strike It Rich* theatre. I sat backstage on an electrician's black box, and watched the brisk technicians and secretaries moving to switches and stepping sharply around equipment. Out front Lee Trust was warming up the ladies.

The electric organ had started now, and I saw people around me looking at the clock. A woman leaned down. Her hair was dyed white-silver. She looked like a female impersonator. Her husky, modulated voice said, "Hi, sweetie, you on the show?"

I nodded to her and looked down again at the hinges on the electrician's black box. The woman went up to watch the cut-in to the network. Supporting her airy silver bubble of hair, she stood looking at the set for a while, then came back to me. Her voice was so close it was like warm water in my ear, droplets, coins. "I wish I could go on, and win prizes so easy."

"Couldn't you?" I felt a pain, an ulcer of sexmoney in my stomach.

She waited a while, destroying cuticles, and then said, "You're adorable, you know?"

I—I love America.

I prowled absently backstage. Rio, Red.

A voice, an electric whisper: "All right, son. Get ready. Stand here. We'll call you out, Warren will bring you on, he'll lead you."

Warren Hull—the Star Himself, I could see his body just beyond the curtain, moving into a million homes.

"And now, ladies and gentlemen, friends of this fine woman who is trying to tear up that mortgage and win back that farm, get her husband off his back, we have selected for you an assistant —"

I could see him, Warren Hull, right there, so close, a few feet away—

"To get that farm back you need a hired hand, someone who can help you with your work and here he is, from Modesto, California, the young man who was just crowned yesterday as the winner of the American Legion's National Oratory Title—young Mr. Danny McCall."

I made my entrance.

I too am now walking into a million homes.

And I shall have to watch it, one week from now, in the privacy of my own home.

A Native Son of The Golden West in the whiteblind lights of the stage.

Smile, you're on Candid Douchebag.

The weary face of the sad rural woman, the smiling Warren Hull, the blank glow of the congregated housewives applauding on cue.

I wanted desperately to do an UnAmerican Activity. What I should do is take it out and pee all over them.

"Come out here, young man, and let America take a look at you."

Smiling glorious, an incarnation of dawn, I went out to shake Warren Hull's hand.

"I've never met you, have I, Dan?"

"No, that's right, Warren."

"Yessir, I never got a chance to meet you backstage, and here is the lady you're going to help—if you can answer the magic questions—Mrs. Edna Murray."

I shook her cold hand. Dumpy, puffy, she was wearing a black dress and a snaky lava rhinestone piece of junk on her saggy left breast. She was from a Valley town, like King City or Turlock or Salinas, one of those towns where you pass a ramshackle farmhouse and know some old woman is in there sitting in a closet with an ax.

"What do you think of New York, Dan?"

I was still looking at Mrs. Murray. I said, "Well, I haven't been here long, Warren." He seemed a little unpleased—if you're such a hotshot speaker, kid, get talking. "So you've been speaking all over this wonderful country of ours."

"Yes, I sure have."

uh

They had told him Mother was with me. They wanted a shot of her in the audience. She stood up, and I watched her on the monitor, a lovely shot of Mom smiling. Warren asked me if she had helped me with my speaking. I said, "Oh, you can do a lot in spite of heredity."

uh

But that's what *Dad* always said when we performed together, at all those Father & Son nights, he always put that little joke in there— but, oh, it was absolutely wrong, it was absolutely *awful* to say that about your *Mother*, on close-up —

I knew it was wrong the moment I said it, and I stood there helpless with helpless Mrs. Murray.

"Well—uh—yes," Warren Hull said, Jesus where in Hell did they get this wise-ass kid? "Now if you can answer some questions for us—the two of you—then Danny, you will have helped Mrs. Murray win back her farm. A little surprise for you, too, Dan, if you can do it." And you can do it, kid, right? You're not going to forget the answers goddammit. "Ready, folks?"

Ready, folks?
Ready, folks?
I nodded.
Mrs. Murray was paralyzed.

"Now here is the first one. What is one word which has a double meaning—both a train, a vehicle to ride in, and someone who trains athletic teams?"

A cardboard clock began ticking its long hand on the cardboard wall. I turned to see the great white finger moving in hysterical stop-action around the dial. "Oh, let me see," I looked down at the anxious woman. I had an impulse, suddenly, just to turn to him and say, 'Excuse me, Warren, your fly is down.'

I coughed.

"That would be, oh that would be," I raised my arms and stammered, "Coach. That's it. *Coach*."

Lee Trust, at the dark side of the stage, kicked his feet and waved his hands to stir up applause from the ladies. Behind him in the wings, Frank was darkly sucking his briar pipe.

Excuse me, Warren, your fly's down and your dude is being eyeballed coast-to-coast.

I stared at Mrs. Murray: year after year of pointless anonymous rural suffering, all frantic and cold sweat dressed up coast to coast for ten noon-hour minutes.

I got to do this for her.

Right?

Right!

My palms began to sweat needles. "Good for you, Dan."

Good for you, Dan.

"Now your next question—what is the capital of Brazil? Take your time, folks. The capital city of Brazil?"

I leaned down to Mrs. Murray. We were conferring. I said to her, "It's Rio. You say it this time. Rio de Janeiro."

Looking at the clock her little face cracked, and Mrs. Edna Murray stuck out her bloated hand and whispered "Rio de Janreuoiw."

With the applause I stared at the monitor facing the stage and saw myself in the small gray light. Haven't we seen you somewhere before?, I scratched my nose and saw in the monitor a gray person scratching his wavelength-pebbles nose.

Warren, your pants are unzipped, oh, oh—please, Warren, you're not going to— to *expose* yourself?

He came between us. "You're half-way to the final jackpot and the farm for the prize. Now take your time on these last two questions, and ponder your answers carefully, because we're coming to the big money."

They had explained to me the red telephone on a block; if we failed, if we forgot, they would ring the telephone—"Heartline to America"—and pretend somebody had just called in and would contribute the money for the prize anyway. Just wait, let it ring, watch Warren say, "Heartline call—Heartline call!"

I know what to do! It'll be a front-page story, the incorruptible American Legion Champ exposes Fixed TV Quiz Show. Before they can stop me, I'll step forward: "Mr. Chairman, The People Shall Be Heard! Ladies and Gentlemen this show is *fixed*—they *give* you the answers!"

What could Warren and Lee and Frank—what *could* they do? I clasped Mrs. Murray's hand.

"Now folks, here's the problem. You'll have double time to name three tunes by George Gershwin. Ready, Go."

Ready, Go?

Ready Go The Fuck Away.

"Well, that could be 'Rhapsody in Blue,' 'Summertime,' and 'Someone To Watch Over Me.' Is that all right?"

You *bet* it is! Lee, watching it all off-camera from the side of the stage, led the audience again in the storm of applause.

"Well, what a wonderful partner you've got there, Mrs. Murray."

The old girl wheezed like a farm animal.

"Yessir, you're doing a fine job, Danny. And if you can answer one last question, we've got a surprise for you. At "Bond's The Clothier"—an entire fall wardrobe for college. With your Mother this very day we'll send you over so you can pick out the shirts and slacks and sports coats—the whole business. OK, Dan?"

Strike It Rich? Strike it *Cheap*!

A Corvette, you fucker, I want a Corvette. You think I'm going to keep silent for neckties and socks?

I looked at the Heartline, the red plastic prop.

"OK, Warren."

"Now the two of you put your heads together for the final answer, and the prizes are yours. Ready?"

I nodded and put my arm around her.

Actually, I'm a good kid. Nobody believes it, but I am.

"Here is the big one: who was the first woman doctor in the United States of America?"

HELP

Jesus, *help*.

I pledge allegiance to Edna Murray and to the Republic for which she stands.

Think, Philbrick, Think. I Led Three Lives. At least!

"No help now, folks." Warren Hull turned to the audience, as if it had the answer on the tip of its great tongue. "The first woman doctor in America."

The lights and cords, black wires sprawled on the apron, nervous systems coiled and running.

Lunge over and French-kiss Warren Hull—Warren's about ready to crack too, and then suddenly he humps back, Cut To Commercial—

In the shadows, a technician was soundlessly shouting instructions to a dolly camera to move up and give armored support. Warren said, "It's a tough one, so take your time." His eyes pleaded with me: Come on, kid, don't make me answer the red telephone, I hate to answer the red telephone. Come on, kid, gimme a break.

David told me it would be dangerous—

My kid brother told me it would be dangerous to do a thing like that, especially on a Sunday. Mom and Dad would be terribly embarrassed. In front of the guests.

But I did it, I did it. I so hated to say the blessing, I hated to bless the food, so I gave them one they'd never forget:

"Almighty and most merciful Father, we beg that thy blessing be upon this food and upon this fine table of guests gathered here. We ask thy blessing upon our loved ones, both here and departed, and beseech thee to give us all a final and beautiful place in thy heavenly home. We pray that we have not sinned in taking this fowl from thy flock, and that by so borrowing it we may enrich our bodies to carry out thy service. We thank thee for this salad and for these vegetables and all the good things of our repast, for we know they come from you, and from Thy Holy Harvest.

"We ask today as we gather for this noon meal a blessing upon all those in our country who are in positions of authority. We ask you to bless the President of the United States, the Vice President of the United States, the Secretary of State of the United States, the Congress—both Senate and House of Representatives—of these United States. We ask you to bless our State, County, and Local Officials, our police department, and all those who are with us in a healthy and continuing regulation of thy affairs in this prosperous country and this heart of happiness in this very home."

David began to snicker like an eight-year old, which he was.

"We ask thy blessing on each country and commonwealth of this world and the resolution of the forces which separate them from a continuing and lasting brotherhood under the light and leadership of thy son, Jesus Christ, brighter surely than any world son or sun of the Heavens. We know that thy grace is over all those who are in sickness, and despair, and sin. And we know that you will heal them in their distress."

All at the table were beginning to stir; father moved his hands at his plate.

"So, Lord, bless us, the food, and the spirit which brings us one to the other."

What time? What time? The time of your life. Four seconds left. Bless us, Almighty God, and lead us in the paths of righteousness.

The first woman doctor in the United States was Ophelia Fingerbang.

Your fly's down and your show's fixed: Heartline to America—

Eagerly Danny asked:

                "Elizabeth Blackwell?"

CHAPTER NINE

A STANFORD MAN

"Education: the path from cocky ignorance to miserable uncertainty."
— Mark Twain

"Maybe I was just tired of being me."
— Sandy Koufax, on why he retired.

"I do not love men: I love what devours them."
— Andre Gide

PART ONE
The Bargain

1957 Fall semester, Freshman year

And then it happened.

I broke my bargain with Gram and Gramps. I smashed it to smithereens.

All semester I felt it coming—everybody at Stanford smoked and drank, all the students and professors. On weekends it seemed like I was the only sober guy in the fraternity I'd pledged, Delta Chi. I knew it was time now. I was a Stanford Man.

At age 18, I lost it, oh Christ, I lost it in Perry Lane, at a TA's "Last Blast" party, in a crazy little toy town just beyond the Stanford golf course. I was taken there by Charley Moyle, my Freshman Advisor, an oddly delicate man with prematurely gray hair, he loved to ride in my brand-new MG. A bunch of beatniks lived in the TA's pad, which Charley called "The Bower of Bliss." The host invited me because I was a promising young man.

Under the evening stars several dozen people roamed around the prim gardens, sprawled in the tiny yards of quaint houses, and gathered around bonfires that blazed low while hi-fi speakers blared out hot jazz. I contributed a five-spot to the guys who were making a last booze run to Whiskey Gulch. I said get me a pint of whiskey (I didn't know the difference between bourbon and scotch).

The booze runners came back, distributed their spoils, and when they came around to me, made their delivery, I took an offered Marlboro. I sat there with it, puffing (I didn't know how to inhale). I poured my first drink, and stared at it for a long time. Then I lifted it to my lips, and broke the bargain. My initial swallow almost blew my head off. How could you even taste it when it set your mouth and throat on fire?—Lord, they ought to pay you *to* drink it. Maybe if I spit it up and threw the rest away, the bargain could still be intact.

I drank carefully, sipping, while I listened to the Bill Evansy cool jazz and watched the others being drunk. Mark Schorer fell around my feet and asked me if I wanted to hear "something funny" and I nodded and he said "I wrote a book about Sinclair Lewis" and I agreed that was pretty funny and then Ian Watt asked me for a light and I forgot I had a pipe lighter and so when I held it up the flame went PA-WOOM and Ian grabbed his nose like a critical article—"OH!"—and a man from Vanderbilt who was my freshman English teacher kept pushing Wallace Stegner down on the couch, bellowing "The South shall rise ahgayn!" and came at me with his home-made beer—Christ, you had to chew it—and he tried that Reb Honeysuckle crap on me at the doorway leading down to the patio and I sidestepped him and down he went, bombity-bomb, never to rise ahgayn, and Ted Tayler dodged him on his way back up pissed because the cops wouldn't let him drive home, "They made me do tricks in their flashlights, goddamn eyeball tricks," and he had tried to focus and dilate but he said to the fuzz, "You got a spider crawling on your shirt," and the cop said, "That's not a spider, shorty, that's a badge," and a pirate—he really looked like a pirate, with a gold earring and a big mustache and beetle juice on his face, and a big live parrot on his shoulder—began calling out, "Anybody around here see my *Self*? I lost it tonight. Reward for return," to which a witch in a black butterfly shirt responded "I envy the fools who know how to care," and—

"I think I will get drunk too," I announced to no one in particular.

That was my last mistake.

From then on I was drinkin' and smokin', smokin' and drinkin', envyin' the fools who know how to care, and I became peculiarly talkative, haranguing people at the bonfire, and then I seemed to be standing *in* the bonfire for a second, and the pirate called me a "flaming faggot," he really snarled at me, and I saw the parrot take wing. The pirate tried to square things between us, he said I misunderstood, you always put faggots in fires, and I said I understood very well, the Supreme Court judges aren't *elected*, and let me tell you about E—liz—a—beth Black—well, and the pirate just looked at me, "what the fuck are you talking about?" Extremely wobbly, I was so angry with myself for breaking my promise to my grandfather, a thousand bucks out the window. I said to the pirate, "I'm talking about talking!" He went away to look for his parrot.

I finished the Jim Beam. And then all the images go round and round:

hanging out the third story window singing over the alley, staggering over to a bunch of people listening to a guy playing guitar, singing "*La Donna e mobile*" at full throttle, ear-splitting, people saying shut up, why don't you get somebody to take you home

Gwen Davis asking me who I was and my saying "A serious writer," and her face going to charcoal bone pulling the hearing aid out of Malcolm Cowley's ear and shouting, "calling all exiles, calling all exiles," and Malcolm glaring at me and saying "you are a dangerous schizophrenic"

picking a fight with Schuler the puke-up-them-guts novelist who hated sensitivity, Goddamn it I broke my promise and now I'm going to break your *face*, and going down with him to the street and throwing a punch and missing completely and falling down

a red-headed guy named Vitzum carting me off to the police station and me shouting "red headed faggot" at him, saying Fuck You Fuck You and Charley trying to get me to go back to the frat and my saying "You sleep with him, you want to, you sleep with him and be a fairy," and Charley begging Vitzum to release me to his custody, and Vitzum finally saying OK

Charley loading me into my MG and driving me back to Delta Chi, where two of my brothers were playing bridge with their dates, and me crashing right through the card table, shouting at one of them, "you're that girl from the cemetery in Eugene!" and telling the other girl she was an "angry virgin," bellowing, "I want some more booorbon, some more PRISHLESH INGREEDYENT"—

When I woke up the next morning something terrible had happened: in the night I had thrown up, straight up into the air, and it had fallen backwards down on top my face and now my eyes were sealed shut with crusted puke.

I crawled blindly to the bathroom, and sat clothed on the shower floor, hot water beating on me.

I dried off, and then Charley Moyle came by to check on me, and he showed me, reminded me, and told me; I couldn't believe it. I what? Then I did what? It sounded stupid and sick. No wonder Gramps didn't want me to drink.

We returned to the scene of my crime; our host was up, and gave us real orange juice. He said everybody would have had a much better time if I hadn't been there. He gazed away murmuring with wonder, "God, what defenses—what defenses you must have." I begged him to tell me everything, where, what, but he had his eye on Charley.

How on earth could I have done such a thing? I thought of telephoning everybody whose name I could find out, to let them know I wasn't like last night, truly not: Dan McCall is not like that at all, I'm—I'm Dr. Jekyll—that, that Mr. Hyde stuff, that was just an act, it was Dramatic Interp, I mean come on—

I slank back to Delta Chi. Most of my brothers thought it was funny: "Man, were you *wack-o*!"

I *was* a Delta Chi brother, and I had earned it painfully: "My name is mucous-masticating mammary-mouthing moss-mumbling monster-mouse masturbatory-McCall o most exalted Active SIR!" During initiation's Hell Week, after forty hours without sleep, painted red white and blue, wearing a gunny sack with a dead fish and an onion hanging around my neck, crammed inside the hearth of the fireplace with three other pledges, scrubbing the flue with our toothbrushes while ice-water was poured down the chimney, the word "masticating" warped in my head and died in my mouth, I couldn't say it in ten seconds and so I reeled and bent and grabbed my balls as the Active laid on with his paddle.

And now it was on to the whorehouse, me and my brothers. Tub Cowley was gettin' together a carload for a trip up to Vallejo, sixty miles away. Well, I done smoked and drunk, so why not? Still though, should I go to a whorehouse—on a Sunday?

Why not, fuckhead?

Six of us went in Cowley's big silver Oldsmobile.

We cruised on up to the Vallejo Greyhound station to a line of sleeping taxis. A door opened, and a voice wheezed out to us:

"Want a ride, men?" Tub went over to ask him about the deal while we stood around looking inconspicuous. Tub came back nodding. "Let's go."

The driver asked, "All you guys twenty one?"

"Sure."

He looked at me. "You're twenty-one?"

I nodded my head. "I'm twenty-two."

He smiled. "Bullshit."

And then we were driving in the cab, brothers, going to get our logs flogged. The cabbie was wearing a faded Hawaiian shirt, blue jeans, and beach sandals. In the light coming down dimly from the dashboard his toes were gray. I leaned up and said "I really am twenty-two. It's funny, I even get asked in liquor stores."

In the backseat Slocum said, "Shut up, McCall."

The driver said, "I got to stop for another car. Can't be seen taking the cab."

We nodded.

We changed cars—got into a black Packard for Christ's sake—and headed out of town.

"You fellows go to Stanford," the cabbie said. He had noticed Tub's jacket. "You've come a long way to get your ashes hauled."

As we went on the street became a road, rough and uneven; our unmarked tank growled along beyond the city lights and into the darkness and rain of the fields. As we passed through the wet jungle I thought back to my public disgrace at the Last Blast Party, and I daydreamed about writing something to tell the guests how sorry I was, to put down on paper some words that would let them know I wasn't like that night, truly not; Dan McCall is not who you think he is, Dan McCall is loving and gentle, in a thousand ways. And Dan McCall is brave, he's there in a crisis, you can count on him. In the backseat I crouched down terrified. Danny McCall is a virgin.

Tub said, "I thought there was a house in town."

"I like to bring the fellas out to Ina's. She's usually got nice girls. The two out here now are up from Hollywood."

"No danger of gettin' rolled?"

"Hell no," the driver chuckled, "no rough stuff. I wouldn't last long that way. There's the boat house, we're almost there." He turned into a slithery lane. At the end of it we pulled up to a farmhouse with a low white light burning at the door.

"Here she is."

We coasted into the muddy driveway and parked beside a beautiful white Vette

Tub said, "Somebody makes money."

"Customer. City official. They all know Ina." He turned off the engine and got out.

That Vette, my beautiful white *Strike It Rich* Vette.

As we went up the door opened, and an older woman— jeez, she looked just like Edna Murray from the show!—said, "Hello, fellahs."

We trooped in, and she said, "Hi, Smitty," to the driver, and then we all stood around like it was the first half-hour of a bad party. Except I knew big men were going to burst out of the shadows, beat me unconscious and take all my money.

Beers were passed around. I drank mine slowly and didn't turn into a madman.

A door opened, a door that had bedrooms behind it, and two women about twenty-five came out in blue cocktail dresses. One was a red-head and the other was a silver-blonde. Edna Murray said, "Boys, meet my girls, Carlene and Sondra."

Everything was electric, a stop. I fixed immediately on the one who looked like Kim Novak.

The other one said, "Who wants to come first?"

Paul took over the lead. "I'm game."

He went in, following Carlene.

Tub took Kim Novak. Sondra. Mine.

And then the rest of us sat around drinking cans of beer, waiting our turn at bat. I tried to be cool and lit a cigarette and was looking at it while I drank beer, but I forgot to pay attention and my mouth didn't fully cover the hole, so some suds ran down my cheek. I backed into the parlor where *Highway Patrol* was on the TV. A little boy was wrapped up in blankets on the couch, a dog asleep on the floor. I went back to my band of brothers. We sat there waiting and thinking. I strolled into the whorehouse kitchen. And suddenly, like magic, Sondra found me there at the sink. She said, "Hey, handsome, you want to come next?"

Smiling, I murmured, "I'm your man."

On the way to the bedroom she said, "You're not in the Navy."

"No, no I'm not..."

She looked at me, as if she was expecting me to say something more.

"No, I've never been in the Navy —"

She waited, smiling.

I thought, But I could tell you about six Navy fliers, whose plane crashed in a rampaging sea—Jesus, Danny Boy, can't you even make conversation?, you of all people, you're all words, and I blurted, "I want to be a writer."

That seemed to please her. "Will you put me in a book someday?"

I promised.

We walked into the bedroom and she shut the door. She said her favorite writer was Tennessee Williams.

Hey, am I supposed to take off my socks or leave them on? I mumbled out a question if she did anything else—I mean, in addition to her career here—

She said she pitched for Singer Sewing Machines. In the summer. They had a softball league.

"Softball?" I had trouble believing that—a prostitute pitching for a women's softball team. But she insisted. She showed me her wind-up, just for fun.

"You got to pay me first, hon'."

"Oh sure, sure. How much?"

"What do you want, honey?"

Well… I looked away. Whadda ya mean what do I

want? Doesn't everybody just—

"Your friend went around the world."

"Tub?"

She seemed confused. "You mean Barry?"

Tub said his name was Barry?

"I can't give her less than twenty, honey."

"Okay." I handed her two ten spots.

While she left to go deposit the money with Edna Murray, I took off my clothes. I jumped on the bed to see if the springs squeaked, but it was hard as a rock.

Sondra with her high-piled platinum hair was all at once with me again, smiling, closing the bedroom door behind her, and BINGO she was out of her dress; she had a Heartline to America, way down there.

Naked. An absolutely naked woman. She made the furniture in the room and the carpet, all warm and shabby and brown, all of the whole world, the visible universe naked and close. The mind and the spheres began to behave.

"Hi."

And then we, she and I, The Real Thing, went into the little dark bathroom, and I looked tremblingly at her naked body, hairless expect for the trail of platinum shards on top. Why didn't she have more hair there? Maybe she had some terrible disease that made it fall out. Or maybe she had shaved it to *prevent* disease. Or maybe—well, now she was washing me, with warm soapy lather. And we chatted once again about Tennessee Williams in particular and writing in general. She was really nice. She was gentle during the rinse cycle. We talked some more about softball—I didn't want her to think that she was just an object, I mean I wanted to know about her life and everything. While she washed my penis I smiled down at it. Changing from Danny Boy to Dangerous Dan.

You are pretty, you are great. "You don't need to do this."

She smiled, "I don't?"

"You could choose your own, couldn't you?"

"It's no fun if you can choose."

We went back into the bedroom, and I stood at the foot of the rock-hard bed, watching her, the white hair on her head on a white spread in a low white light.

"What you waitin' for, honey?"

I just—I mean, I feel so bad about breaking my bargain, I let the family down.

"C'mere, hon—" She held her lovely arms up, completely nude, more like a bride than a whore.

So I lay down and hugged her, and we rolled around. She laughed and played in my hair with her fingers, she whispered a few words, and reached down and put me inside her.

And then we were fucking.

Really.

For a long time.

At one point she said, "Easy, baby, we'll break its back."

I slowed down immediately, like taking your foot off the gas when you see a cop.

But after a bit we went back into high and we were tearing along again, her vocabulary went all to pieces, she was sighing and whimpering in my ear—

Yes. Fine. Everything fine.

"*Hon*-ey?"

Yes? I was trying to keep my weight on my elbows and knees, but Sondra pushed me on my left shoulder, and looked hard into my eyes. "What's the matter, honey?"

Excuse me?

"You're not drunk —"

No, not *now*—

"Why didn't you come, honey?" To make absolutely sure, she pulled me out and looked me over. She sat there holding onto me. "You *didn't* come, did you?"

I panicked; I whispered, "Well, I don't know —"

"You don't *know*?"

Well, I, I mean—why was she pissed off at me? I patted the bed with my hand. "I guess I did." I looked at the wallpaper. I'll probably dream about this wallpaper for the rest of my life.

"Hey," she touched my naked shoulder, "hey—look at him." My eyes boggled to the door—I thought someone was coming in on us—

And then I understood. Oh, *him*—I looked down at him.

"You *didn't* come, sweetie."

Well sometimes I do, and then there are other times, you know—

"Let me French." She leaned over and put him in her mouth.

oh

I leaned back on my elbows and scanned her silver hair. She wasn't like Kim Novak at all; she was Sondra, peppy, she had school spirit.

And now she made a lot of stagey moans, and talked away with her mouth full, she put her arms around my back and pulled me forward so that my stomach would sort of bump into her hair a little.

I wanted to help in any way possible, I dug my feet in down below, and put my hands down beside her, I lifted myself slightly up, I didn't want to choke her, but it was such a great feeling, it made me happy, like the first entrance on my unicycle at a big formal banquet—like God built you to do it—and she began to sway her head from side to side—

and then something was happening to me, maybe she was breaking something, I couldn't stand it anymore, wait look out, something's gone wrong —

I felt it—

almost painful, way down deep, a sudden tightening, when you know you're asleep but you also know you are about to wake up, and then you fight to stay down there in your sleep because you love the dream you're having—

I UNDERSTOOD—

BEFORE IT HAPPENED—

what happens next is

painful—

LOOK OUT

shit it hurts, a traveling explosion, it *hurtles*—

Sondra grinned and popped me out of her mouth—

oh shit, *help*—

HELP—

Sondra grabbed my cock, wide-eyed I watched it happen, terrified and glad—

again—

again—

and Sondra gave him another sweet pull and he—

oh me, oh ME—

"*There,*" she said, "*There* you are, hon!"

Jesus, I came in the air—

Great God in Heaven, of *course*—YOU DON'T HAVE TO BE ASLEEP, I COULD HAVE BEEN DOIN' THIS FOR *YEARS*!

She was bustling at the walnut dresser. I put one sock on and was ready with the other, standing on one foot, balanced on one leg like a tall bird in water, when I felt called upon by her close breathing silence.

"Here, honey, let me clean your gun."

"Excuse me?"

She gently grabbed my used-penis and stuck a long silver needle into it, just a little.

Pay no attention.

A needle in the hole itself, and she squirted something in there, like Penicillin. It didn't hurt.

She was getting into her dress. "I don't know how you college guys stand it without pussy."

Why the hell didn't anybody *tell* me? Why couldn't someone have been *specific*? Nobody said you could be awake. I'd had nine thousand hard-on's but I just never knew what to *go* for. I always thought—oh fuck what I thought, can we do it again? I've only got $15 left, but Paul's loaded, he'll lend me—

Okay, everything's fine—gee, *thanks*, Sondra—

Bitchin'!

I KNOW NOW— I know now I know now— I KNOW NOW IT IS THE SIMPLEST THING IN THE WORLD—I KNOW NOW—

She helped me with my Stanford jacket, and I went out to the parlor where Smitty was playing gin rummy with Edna Murray. The cold gray glare of the television still sprayed on the little boy and the dog.

Reis said to me, "You took your time. You fall asleep in there?"

On the way back to the bus station in Vallejo, we quarreled a little bit about whether we each owed Smitty a buck or two bucks. We gave him seven dollars, and he seemed happy with that. "Anytime, Gentlemen," he said, standing there in his sandals in the rain. "You can find me here any day except Wednesdays and Sundays."

If we are killed on the highway going back to Stanford, I thought, Danny Boy won't have lived in vain.

PART TWO
I'm Going to be a Writer

1957-1961, Stanford University

My freshman advisor Charley Moyle was extremely interested in my adventure with Sondra. I described it to him in explicit detail. Yes, in spite of a thousand wet dreams, going all the way back to that plane ride with Mother coming home from Louisville, somehow I'd never consciously ejaculated before. Charley laughed, "You didn't need to, Danny Boy. All those years up on that unicycle, you know what you were doing?"

"What?"

"Masturbating. Up there in front of all your audiences. You were jacking off to everybody."

"*What?*"

He added, "Don't you see the wonder of it? You were so alienated, you were estranged even from your own body!"

So one night when my roomie was home in Woodside cramming for exams, I looked down at the big bulge in my pajamas, and I tried it, on my own and it was so easy, the easiest thing in God's beautiful world. I wiped up with a sock. Maybe I'm one in a million. Maybe I'm the only one in the history of mankind. Your first orgasm in a prostitute's mouth? How many guys could say that? I lay there utterly satisfied. Then—

I did it again, it was like a dance-step, once you 'get it', you better imprint it, practice the perfect feeling. It was a thrill of accomplishment, that that milky fluid on my heart and wrist, I turned on the light to look again, smell, taste. What an ecstasy of understanding!

Still, it wasn't absolutely right. In some sense I was still a Virgin. It was in her mouth, not the real place—still a virgin, it bothered me, like cheating on a biology exam. The next morning after a masturbatory quickie I decided I'd go back and do it proper with the other girl at the whorehouse, Carlene. So I did. Carlene was sullen and tired. It wasn't terrific at all, I shot off five seconds after I went in.

In the kitchen, Sondra said, "Hi, stranger."

I went all alone. Without the brothers. Then I went to *A Streetcar Named Desire* in Berkeley, and hung around on Telegraph Avenue before driving home, unhappy, back to Delta Chi.

My frat brothers thought the courses I took were effeminate. Delta Chi was full of pre-meds and ROTC studs and Electrical Engineering illiterates, and they loved to taunt me by asking all girlishly how things were going in "The New England Renaissance" and "Early Tudor Lyric" and "British Wit and Humour." But I loved the books. I was glued to *Sons and Lovers*, and couldn't figure out how D. H. Lawrence knew my mother. I read *David Copperfield*—how did Dickens make that whole world? I read *The Sun Also Rises* in one sitting, up in my room, from noon to midnight. In Modesto High I'd read only one novel, *The Red Badge of Courage*, because it was the shortest book on the required list.

I made mistakes, of course. The San Francisco State Drama Department put on their prize-winning production of *Waiting For Godot*, and I laughed myself silly, but a couple of people in the audience looked at me with stern disapproval and shook their heads. How could I laugh at a masterpiece of existentialism? But then my freshman advisor Charley Moyle told me I was right—*Godot* is, indeed, hysterically funny. So I was right the first time. At least I could see, at the Sunday night "flicks," that *Citizen Kane* was the greatest movie ever made. Stanford was changing my life. It felt like I was learning something new and deep every single day.

The summer after my freshman year, having just discovered books, I decided I wanted them all. Starved, I stuffed myself with anything; in a week I would read *The Death of Ivan Ilych*, *Look Homeward, Angel*, *Vile Bodies*, *Cannery Row*, and *Persuasion*.

The fall of '59 in my sophomore year I took a course from Yvor Winters, the reclusive star of the English Department, who was a tough critic. He had written on one student's term paper, "There is a limit to which the obvious can be insisted upon with any degree of effectiveness." On a poor young woman's portfolio of poems he wrote, "You have absolutely no talent." And once he had growled at me, observing me on my unicycle (a bad idea), "I see the circus is in town."

I loved Winters' lectures on Herman Melville. He had acquired one of Melville's own harpoons, and held that harpoon over his head for the whole 50 minutes of his first lecture on *Moby Dick*. I went back to Delta Chi, and I tried reading *Moby Dick* while holding a nine iron over my head—I could barely do *that* for 50 minutes. One day I sat in the library, not bothering to eat, and read two great short novels by Melville: *Billy Budd*—God Bless Captain Vere—and *Bartleby, The Scrivener*. I lost myself in the magnificent isolation of Bartleby, he was my main man. "I prefer not to." During all those Contest days, how come I never said that?

I read Hawthorne, and saw that he was frightened, grieved that the "life . . . life . . . life" was always out of reach, always escaping him, and he found himself alone in America, "uttering vague masses of talk," crying, "I have not lived but only dreamed about living," finding himself cut off from the common labors of people, "a citizen of somewhere else."

The grad students' bible was Winters' famous book, *In Defense of Reason*. So I spent an afternoon in my room on the third deck of Delta Chi and carefully worked out a limerick:

> Mr. Winters whose heart has its reason
> Let it slip just for once into treason —
>   In moral commotion
>   He defended emotion,
> And fell straight to hell for that reason.

There! I took it to his office where he sat sullenly smoking his pipe, and I gave it to him. He glared at me, picked it up, read it, and then kept on glaring at me. Then his iron mask changed, a new light came into his eyes, and he began to laugh. And he didn't give it back to me, he kept it.

In the spring I started going with an ugly girl. That's what the brothers said she was—"Hey, McCall, is tonight pig night again?" She was fat and unkempt (my concerned roommate posed the uncivil question, 'If she can't stop eating, couldn't she at least buy a comb?') The graduate students in English called her the Duchess of Menlo.

She was very lovely. At first I thought maybe her reading was as unsystematic and frantic as mine— she indicated a love for both *Sister Carrie* and *To the Lighthouse*. But I gradually found out that she loved those two books simply because she loved them; she wasn't making lists of the "Ten Best" like I was. I'd heard that Dreiser wrote like a hippopotamus, and said so; she just shook her head and said flatly, "It holds up." Somebody told me Mr. Winters dismissed "the iridescent trifling of Mrs. Woolf"; I thought it was clever so I quoted it to her. Duchess said, "Aw, Uncle Tits doesn't scare me."

At another beatnik party in The Bower, I was fastidiously bright and quiet, holding my liquor, and then suddenly Duchess and I were in a little bedroom fucking on coats to a Bessie Smith record. Afterwards we avoided each other for an hour. At 2:30 she caught me in my Stanford jacket at the door and leaned against me: "I don't want you to go."

Of course I never took her to fraternity parties, but I did fuck her in the fraternity house.

It was astonishing – she *liked* to do it. After watching *The Seventh Seal* I stopped my MG by the old post office and said, "Left" (back to your dorm) or "Right?" (Delta Chi for a screw). She looked at me strangely, then gazed at nothing and said, trying to laugh, "Oh, hang a right."

Naked together on my bed, I read her a story I had written about us fucking. I could tell she didn't like it. I liked it, it gave me a hard on. She wondered where I *did* get the notion that I lived at the center of the universe. If it were not so, I said, they wouldn't have told me. I gave my lively sunshine stories and my moonlight fears, both, to Duchess. She was pleased with my progress and said, "McCall"—she always called me by my last name—"McCall, you have the makings of an amateur."

She rolled like Moby Dick on my bedsheets. I touched her and she touched me. I got a hysterical erection when she played with nipples. She said it was a shame that most men didn't know how sensitive their nipples were; she said they were too busy mauling the woman's boobs. I asked her how many men she had slept with.

I thought she'd say half a dozen, anyway.

She said one, besides you.

I asked her how she knew so much, then, about men.

She said she read a lot.

After parties I'd always ask her how I had been. She seemed irritated. Some people thought college courses shouldn't be graded; she said mine should. She said my life should. After we fucked she looked at me. "B+."

One night after we finished I found that the stupid prophylactic had never got on right, it was pasted against her thigh, and as we dressed she had tears on her cheeks. I was afraid she was pregnant and asked her why she was crying. She said, "McCall, I don't think I want to feel about you the way I do." Then she composed herself, and stood there like Falstaff in her bra and shrugged. She sighed. "What's nice about not having dignity is that you can't lose it."

At school I still loved my teachers, and they seemed to like me. Bill Wiegand, the prize-winning novelist and critic, said my short story about a frightened little boy alone in the night was "beautifully put together," and he passed it on to his literary agent who sold it to *Redbook* for $750. Not in the American Legion neighborhood, money-wise, but a start. Winters taught me Hawthorne's little masterpiece "The Hollow of the Three Hills," and in another course Tom Arp taught Emily Dickinson's great poem "I felt a Funeral, in my Brain." And suddenly I saw they were the same experience! A dozen big and little things in common—the tragic young lady, the tolling death-bell, the coffin. I handed in my term paper, and found that neither Arp nor Winters knew about all the connections. So I sent my discovery to the *New England Quarterly*, and they published it. Hey, maybe I could do this for a living. In my high school oration for the Native Sons of the Golden West I quoted some guy who said "Find something you love and you'll never work a day in your life." OK. I love this. Teaching literature would be no way to Strike It Rich, but it's really interesting, and you'd have lots of free time to get drunk.

Charley Moyle got us two tickets for the matinee showing of *Long Day's Journey Into Night* in San Francisco, and we drove up in my MG. The performance blew us away, and at the first intermission Charley went to a liquor store and bought us a pint of bourbon. At the second intermission we were so devastated that we traded hits from the bottle in the parking lot beside the MG. The whole tragedy of *family*. Frederick March and his wife, Florence Eldridge—oh, when he stood on the stairs, her old wedding dress in his arms! Back at Delta Chi,

Charley and I finished off the bottle, we couldn't get over the emotional hurricane we'd been through.

In the dining room at Delta Chi, I went berserk. Starting around ten p.m., I did all my orations, a mad speech contest. Where's my unicycle? Guess who's here—Danny Boy! Goddamit, am I ever going to get over who I was? I know, I know, I'm drunk, but I can still do it, and I'll prove it to you right here, move back, people, give me some room—I gave "Optimism for Courageous Living," The Lion's Club "Youth's Promise for Tomorrow's World," the Alexander Hamilton Bi-Centennial Address, the Native Sons of the Golden West, the American Legion triumph on the Constitution. I did them absolutely straight, not a hint of parody, I was alive in my past perfection, I did Biff and Willy Loman, I did Cyrano, I even gave a sermon I wrote for Youth Day at the First Methodist Church in Modesto. But I felt a sharp pang of remorse: what was I doing? Was I flushing Dad's *Fundamentals of Speech* down the toilet? I couldn't help it, all the speeches came cascading down like an avalanche. My Delta Chi brothers would take a break from studying for exams, they'd come down to refill their coffee mugs, they'd sit for a few minutes and listen and smile and shake their heads—

When I woke up on the couch the next morning (someone had put a blanket over me like a shroud) I had a brutal hangover. I called Charley and went over to his apartment for brunch.

Charley came down in a ridiculous red nightshirt to fix coffee. The coffee burned my mouth. The *San Francisco Chronicle* banged against the front door. Charley went in his scarlet nightshirt, skinny bare legs and all, to get it.

"Dan, one of the speeches you gave last night —"

Christ, I'd forgotten—Charley stayed for the speeches? Drinking is not a good idea.

Charley continued, "Worldwide, millions of children die of starvation every year—and you still believe that 'the order of the universe is designed to produce the greatest good'?"

Shit, I couldn't seem to remember anything—how many speeches did I do last night? Apparently I gave the Optimist oration.

He stood there with the *Chronicle* in his hand, looking down at me.

"Well, uh, no. When I came to Stanford, I promised myself I wouldn't let this place take away my faith. But in "Introduction to Philosophy" we had to read *Dialogues Concerning Natural Religion*. And David Hume took all my cherished beliefs, one by one, and smashed 'em to shit. But I gave that speech when I was twelve years old, and I believed it then."

"What about all the cornpone Americana?"

Lamely I muttered, "The Declaration of Independence and the Constitution are not cornpone."

Charley shook his head quietly. "Your parents must have been monsters."

Monsters?! I was speechless.

"You still feel the golden aura of all those trophies and the magic sound of applause and the love from good ol' Ma and Pa that you bathed in. Why did your parents push you so damn hard? Don't you see how your childhood experience fucked you up in some profound way?"

His voice was calm but deadly. He said it again. "Your parents were monsters."

Hey, why aren't we talking about the knockout we saw yesterday, *Long Day's Journey Into Night*? Or are we?

I couldn't take it. "Charley, don't you tell me what my parents *were*. Like they were dead. And they weren't Stage Mothers, I wasn't the dream they were denied, I was the dream they had fulfilled."

"Dan, just listen to you —"

"Cut it out. They *are* and they do—they're leaders of the community."

Charley rolled his eyes.

I rose up in my chair. "Charley, you taught us *Huckleberry Finn*."

"Yes, of course."

"And you said my paper on *Huck* was the best in the class."

"Yes, it was."

"Well where do you think I got it?"

"Excuse me?"

"From my parents. They read the book to me when I was ten. A couple of chapters at bedtime every night. They took turns—my father, my mother, those 'monsters'—in our house at 1259 East 22nd Street in Eugene."

"I see."

"No you don't. My parents helped me to understand the rhythms of speech, language—everything that so impressed you in my *Huck* paper. Shit, Charley, those 'monsters' as you call them—they *taught* me, long before you did. Why is achievement sickness? I learned so much from my parents. Still do. They're very powerful people, sensitive, smart —"

He was just staring at me.

Charley got up from the table and went into the kitchen to make brunch. Man, he was an excellent cook.

Cutting into his western omelet he asked, "So what was your hairstyle in high school? I guess you didn't have a crewcut."

"Mom said my hair was my 'crowning glory'."

"I'm sure she did," he grinned.

In spite of myself I smiled back.

Afterward, with our cigarettes, Charley leaned in and looked at me through the Marlboro smoke. "So—did you ever lose?"

"Yes, a couple times. Spring of my junior year was a terrible defeat."

"Tell me about it."

"The State Finals of the American Legion Oratory Contest. Two legionnaires from Modesto Post 74 drove me down to Los Angeles the night before, and I guess I didn't get enough sleep, didn't do well in the extemp part, and I wound up a humiliating *third*."

"Oh, horror."

I let it go. "We drove back to Modesto that night. I cried all the way, in the back seat. I didn't even go in with them when they stopped for coffee and pie in Bakersfield. At home Mom and Dad couldn't understand it. They said wait until next year. And the next year I won the National Championship. But at the time—I couldn't deal with it at all. Not to win was like an inability to *breathe*."

"Exactly," he said. Charley looked as if somehow

he'd made an important point. Charley sighed, "Dan, I'm afraid you still just want to 'Strike It Rich'."

Shit, did I carry on about that last night, too?

"I've thought a lot about that show. For me, it wasn't about money. It was Win the Trophy—be the *best*. It wasn't a price tag, it was glory. Shit Charley, maybe you're right, maybe I did think anything's okay if you win. But 'Strike It Rich' meant love me, not pay me."

Charley was really looking at me now. "Did you ever tell your parents about 'the fix'?"

"No. I wanted to. But I couldn't. Too ashamed."

Charley waited, then: "Maybe you were afraid that 'the fix' meant that your whole career had something phony about it."

"Maybe."

"You saw through the fakery of winning at all costs."

"Maybe."

"You say you just wanted people to love you." He sighed. And stood up. "Well, *I* love you." He slowly walked around the breakfast table, his eyes locked with mine, and then he put his arms out to my shoulders, slowly pulled me up, and kissed me. Deeply. On the mouth!

I lurched back a couple of steps. "No— no—hey, I'm sorry —"

"It's not your fault that I love you."

Oh, Jesus. He looked so sad in his flaming nightshirt. He pleaded with me. "Oh, Danny —"

It is my fault. I always miss the point.

I went out and got into my MG, the feel of his day's growth of beard scratchy on my cheek.

The next night I took a nap and slept through dinner, so I went to Rudolfo's for a pizza. I took along the slim novel assigned for my Reading of Fiction course. At midnight there I still was, the red candle burnt down, an empty bottle of wine and crusts of pizza on the silver pan on the red and white checkerboard tablecloth. *The Great Gatsby* was the best novel I'd ever read. I didn't go straight back to the fraternity, I drove around the Palo Alto hills in the moonlight, sitting in the crimson leather seat of my MG, the tires biting into the sandy pavement. I drove and drove, seeking "something commensurate to [my] capacity for wonder," as "…the dark fields of the republic rolled on under the night…. And one fine morning" —

Yes, I'm going to be a writer.

CHAPTER TEN

HOME AGAIN

"They fuck you up, your mum and dad.
They may not mean to, but they do."
— Philip Larkin, "This Be The Verse"

"'You shouldn't complain,' Ursula told her husband. 'Children inherit their parents' madness.'"
—Gabriel Garcia Marquez,
One Hundred Years of Solitude

June 1961, Palm Desert

During my senior year at Stanford the McCalls had moved from the San Joaquin Valley down to the Coachella Valley, where Dad was the founding president of the College of the Desert. He was building it from the sand up. Mom and Dad and David were living in a big white mansion on a little island of immaculately manicured grass in the middle of a 160-acre parcel of land where construction was in full swing. Freshly graduated from Stanford, I was 21 and David was 14, the youngest Eagle Scout in the history of desert scouting. I had been elected a Danforth Fellow, a four year free-ride through graduate school. Danforth was for "Outstanding Scholars with Religious Convictions."

Mother and Dad said they wanted to give their All-American Champ an opportunity to explore the big wide world. So as a graduation present, they'd give me round-trip airfare to two cities of my choosing, anywhere on the globe. They hinted I couldn't pass up London, I'd love it. And Uncle Frank said I should see something entirely new and different—Calcutta would be an experience I'd never forget. In June I could stay with the folks in Palm Desert for a while, and later in the summer I would head overseas for my London/Calcutta trip. Then in September I would return to the States to attend Columbia in the Big Apple.

David had grown at least five inches the past year; he was Mr. Cool, lanky and lean, with short-cropped white-blonde hair. And there he stood in uniform, with a sash full of badges, at an awards ceremony in Indian Wells with Dwight Eisenhower, Ike, turning his famous grin toward the Scouts, my kid brother standing there beaming.

After the ceremony, David took me down by a big date garden to show me a little corral where he kept his palomino horse, Apollo, a frisky little filly with a snow-white mane and tail. I watched as David took her galloping over the sand dunes. She bucked, and David's head snapped back a bit, I saw a patch of blue sky between his butt and her saddle—I hollered, "Stay with her, kid!" and he did, away they went down into an arroyo.

Next morning in bed in "The White House," still dreamy, I heard it:

> "In *Time* magazine in 1944, at the time of the battle of Attu, there appeared a dramatic story of gallantry and tragedy. Six Navy fliers…"

I shook my head into the pillow. Mom and Dad were playing the record of my old Optimist Victory Speech, a little joke to welcome Danny Boy home. But I listened to it in my half-sleep, and the voice was lower, a little peculiar, the inflections weren't right and the timing was off. That's not me! I certainly don't remember it *that* way.

I got up, wrapped my old red robe around me, and wandered down the long hall into the big blue living room. Mother and father were sitting there, with David standing barefoot in white tennis shorts doing my 1952 Optimist Oration, the priceless ingredient, Harry Emerson Fosdick, every paragraph. My heart sank and I slumped into the green rocking chair.

Here we go again.

When David was done, Mother and Dad looked at me.

Silence. The low hum of the air-conditioning.

Dave beat a retreat to his room upstairs.

I was unenthusiastic. I didn't think he should be doing it.

Dad said, "Oh, you think you're the only one who can do it right."

I said no of course not.

The sunlight streaming in the huge windows.

"Well," Mother said, "David's just beginning…"

I looked at her.

Dad said, "Don't sell your kid brother short."

Mother leaned forward and asked why *was* I so negative? Couldn't David at least *try* the Optimist Oration?

They didn't get it. They looked at me, Stanford Phi Beta Kappa Danny Danforth Fellow. I guess the expression on my face gave me away.

I said, "I don't know about ol' David, maybe I'm wrong, but I just don't want you to do it to him, too"—but I stopped when I saw Mother's immensely painful blue eyes.

I turned away, suffused with terrible shame.

A few days later, in *The Palm Desert Post*:

"Inspire children, don't force them, says California Mother of the Year"

The McCalls have two sons, Dan and David, who have been to date just about all any parents could hope for. The younger brother is determined to surpass even the achievements of the older, and may very well do so.

Pictured above in the residence of the President of College of the Desert, the family whose cup of accomplishment runneth over. The White House, as it is called, is bright and cheerful. It overlooks a large expanse of lawn leading to the campus and is separated from the college buildings by tall oleanders.

The living room walls are a pale shade of blue and there are many English antique pieces and wine-colored fabrics. There is a baby grand piano in one corner and a bookshelf above a Victorian loveseat, shelves lined with encyclopedias, a collection of the writings of Fireside Poets and other classics. Fresh roses are in a vase and the candy and nut dishes are filled—as if always ready for a student or faculty member to drop by.

In The Family Room stand shelves of trophies that son Dan won for public speaking. Those won by son Dave will undoubtedly soon join them.

Their mother, Velma, has been selected California Mother of the Year, and frequently travels throughout the state with Mamie Eisenhower. Recently a gala reception was hosted by the TV star Steve Allen.

Ms. McCall says a mother's most important role is as a teacher—inspiring, not demanding or pushing—but leading.

David asked me to take him to the next American Legion meeting in Palm Springs, so the two of us drove up together and parked my MG in front of Legion Hall. It was a low one-story structure of white brick, surrounded by high dusty oleanders; in the front yard a surplus anti-aircraft gun sat spiked down on the crew-cut putting green. Sleek gray, at a forty-five degree angle, the yards-long barrel was pricking the evening sky above 'San Jack.' [3]

David and I went into the hall and past a sleazy little bar where a dozen men and a scattering of wives were hooked up on bar stools, and the cigarette and cigar smoke was thick under the low ceiling in the faint yellow light. The men were wearing their Vet caps with the little medals hanging down, clickety-click, and two of them were drinking in metal wheel chairs, pulled up to the bar like golf carts. Four men were passing among them a single cue, and one man who shot well had only one arm.

We went on into the assembly room where the projector was set up. The Sheriff, a large man with a florid face and bulbous nose, dressed in plain clothes but with a Legion cap, announced the showing of the HUAC movie "Operation Abolition."[4] After the Pledge,

3 San Jacinto Peak
4 Propaganda film alleging Communist conspiracies during student protests.

the Sheriff explained that this movie was an object lesson, it exposed a typical example of Communist deceit, and we were in the ring with Rocky Marciano and we had one hand tied behind our backs. We should watch closely for a few college Jokers from Stanford and Berkeley who were the ring-leaders. They wanted to disrupt the work of the House Committee on Un-American Activities. The Sheriff said he had shown this little movie over forty times to various civic and patriotic groups in the Inland Empire, he knew it inside and out. The house lights dimmed. The real high spot—when the Sheriff wasn't interrupting, "Keep your eyes on *that* Joker, we'll see more of him"—was when the students used lunch-trays to slide on their fannies down the City Hall steps. They all had a good laugh.

When it was over the Sheriff said this was kind of a swan song, he was retiring, but he wanted to emphasize that in dealing with the Communists it wouldn't bother him to put shotguns to their heads. He would receive questions.

One man wanted to know how to fight the Communist Conspiracy in their own communities. The Sheriff said education. In answer to another question he said that an anti-communist certainly did not mean the same thing as a right-wing extremist, and nobody yet had been able to tell him what a right-wing extremist was. Am *I* a Right-Wing Extremist, he wanted to know, are *you*? And he wondered if you were a right-wing extremist just because you campaigned against Open Housing. A man has a right to decide who should be allowed—

A short, stocky dark man across the aisle from

David and me stood up. He was Italian, wearing a gray suit and a red sport shirt and a string tie. In his thick accent he said, "What you mean, people 'should not be allowed'—should not be allowed to live where they want?" He spread his feet and leaned on the empty folding chair in front of him. "You don't believe in the Bill of Rights if you say that."

There was grumbling all around us. A wife with a pocked face glowered at the Italian man, "Freedom of speech does not include the right to yell 'Fire' in a crowded auditorium."

The Sheriff smiled. "Now that little lady has done her homework."

The Italian man was still leaning on his chair. "And you call yourself a Sheriff."

The man who called himself a Sheriff said, "Some of the lip-flappin' these days tries to turn the Bill of Rights into a Bill of Goods. But we're not here to make speeches. I'll do my best to answer any other questions."

The Italian man wouldn't give ground. "I got a question for you, what you do when people shut out somebody from their neighborhood?"

"Law enforcement," the Sheriff growled, "is everybody's business."

Mom's Pastoral Selection Committee still hadn't found a minister for the Palm Desert Community Church, and other pulpits were empty in the blasting heat of the desert. One afternoon Mother handed me a note:

> The Pastor's Study
> First Methodist Church of Modesto

Dear Dan,

You've been winning so many honors that I'm way behind in congratulations. But here's a big one to cover them all. Dan, don't overlook the possibilities for service and for the full use of your unusual talents in the ministry. Your sense of humor brings out the smiles we so often tuck away in a hard world. Drama is coming to the front fast in the Church—Union Seminary in New York is this year calling to its faculty one of America's leading dramatists.

The enduring truth, if it is to be known and received, must be presented to your generation in an intelligent and appealing manner. Drama and dramatic preaching is the most effective mode. Truth requires also the light touch of fancy and humor. These talents you possess in extra-ordinary degree. I believe therefore in the church you might find a place for the shining of your star, and in so doing be a most effective instrument for God in portrayal of His vital, lifting, saving and gracious truth.

I've been wanting to ask you for some time if you could give us a few sermons. How about it? God bless and use you,
Sincerely,
Alan Goozee

One look into Mother's eyes and I knew I couldn't say

no. So the next Sunday I drove from pulpit to pulpit: the 9:30 service in Rancho Mirage and the 11:00 in Cathedral City, the following Sunday I did the 9:30 in Coachella and the 11:00 in Indio. I was all over the place. I had to select the hymns, do the pastoral prayer, preach the sermon: $50 a service, a hundred bucks a Sunday. I was trying to quit smoking, but before preaching I absolutely had to have one. I'd sit in a little stall in the Men's Room, sucking a Pall Mall in the burning heat, going over "Confessions of Our Sins." I pulled a Harry Emerson Fosdick, and asked "Shall the Fundamentalists Win?," read from Jonathan Edwards "Sinners in the Hands of an Angry God," showed how far we had come from that. Mom and Dad had to make courtesy calls at all the churches to drum up support for the College, so I could count on Dad to help out a little, like reading the Scripture Lesson while I'd sit catching my breath in the minister's throne, trying to look Holy.

A couple of weeks later I went out to the mailbox to find a letter from the legendary football coach, Amos Alonzo Stagg:

127 West Euclid
Stockton, California

Dear Dan,
Recently I had a big surprise when I received a copy of your sermon. I am indebted to your minister, Reverend Alan Goozee, who wrote to me that you are also teaching a boys' Sunday School class.

We greatly enjoyed your sermon and were thankful to learn that you are lending your time and effort to helping other youth on the pathway of life. Mrs. Stagg and I are very proud of you.

Heartiest congratulations on your great victories in speaking. It warms the hearts of all your friends. Also warmest congratulations to your parents. I never have bet a cent or a cookie in my life but I am guessing that if I had had equally gifted parents to yours, I would have turned out to be a minister as I had planned instead of an athletic coach.

However, I had a bit of comfort on my hundredth birthday, when the Fellowship of Christian Athletes dedicated the opening session of their conference in Estes Park in my honor and sent me the Revised Standard Version of the New Testament with the following words in gold letters on the cover:

"To Amos Alonzo Stagg, In Recognition of a Christian Ministry in the World of Sport."

Did I ever send you a copy of *Touchdown*? If I did not, I would be glad to give you one. Possibly you might enjoy reading some of the chapters.

Give our love to your dear Father and Mother. Having been an up-to-my-neck football coach for 68 years, you will understand when I say, Keep a level head, Dan, and keep close to the Master.

Sincerely,
Amos Alonzo Stagg
P.S. Please do not bother to acknowledge.

After one bright Sunday service at the Palm Desert Church, I asked the folks who that vision of loveliness was. Well, she was Miss Coachella Valley. She hadn't liked "the atmosphere" at UCLA, and she was going to be one of the few first-year-sophomores at College of the Desert. I called her up. It was quite clear why she didn't like "the atmosphere" at UCLA; she was dumb as a cactus. But her tawny blonde body was everything a Danforth Fellow could ask for in the back seat of the pink Fleetwood parked on the Wildlife Game Preserve just beyond The Smoke Tree Dude Ranch. Her family was Mormon on one side, Christian Science on the other, and she regaled me with her vision of Heaven where her dear dead puppy was romping with angels in cloud-land. I put my Creeping Latitudinarian hands under Miss Coachella Valley's perfectly molded buns, and we experienced God's greatest gift to mankind. Then we strolled naked (except for footwear, there was the danger of sidewinders) on the desert floor, a hundred degrees at midnight. I stood there bare-assed in my gold cowboy boots and stared at her nude body in three-inch peppermint heels, her blonde mind working like a toy.

Dad was hosting a fundraiser for the College of the Desert, a group of Coachella Valley farmers were coming down to make a donation at a dinner hosted by the Shadow Mountain Club. Dad asked me to deliver one of my sermons, an inspiring oration for the guests, and I said I was happy to do it. Gram and Gramps drove down from Redlands to hear it; they were in their eighties now and beginning to fail, but Gramps could still drive; every two years he bought a new red Coupe de Ville. As we all sat at the head table in the Shadow Mountain Club, I had a brief disagreement with Gramps, he had brought me a copy of Barry Goldwater's book, *The Conscience of a Conservative*. I was unappreciative; I said, "If that man is elected President, he'll ruin the country!" Evenly and with perfect imperturbability my bald grandfather said to his salad, "Lots of people say that."

After dinner, President Roy McCall introduced his golden boy, he said it had been hard enough to be known as Velma's husband, but now it was even harder to be known as Danny's father. After my oration there was a lively question-and-answer session; I was self-assured, droll at the mike. I enjoyed the hell out of it. A big man in his late sixties, gorgeously tanned, stood up in the audience and said, "I think you're missing your calling. Why do you want to be a *writer*? You should be a politician, or a preacher."

An odd thing popped into my head: I told them about the National Finals of the American Legion Oratory Contest at Waterville, when I'd mixed up X with XX—I was never much on *substance*. I told the Farmers how the American Legion official had brought Mom up onto the stage, and I'd whispered to her, "I didn't *say* anything" and Mom had whispered back, clasping my hand, "Oh, Danny, none of you said anything—but you said it first!"

The Farmers and their wives found that very funny; in their laughter I looked down the head table at Mom, and she gaily waved at me.

Afterwards, back in The White House, the whole family crowded around in the big blue living room, and Gramps presented me with a check for $1,000. I heard Dad sigh, "Uh-oh."

I stood there, the focus of attention. I said I couldn't take it. No, I said, I'd had to experiment, alas, as teen-agers seem always to have to do. I didn't keep the bargain. I was remembering the Christmas night all those years ago when I signed the pledge. And that crazy shit about swallowing the marble.

My Grandmother, plump on the piano bench, said, "Then we want you to have it for being honest."

Honest? *Honest* is one thing I've never been.

Gramps said he couldn't imagine being prouder of a grandson than he had been of me tonight in the Shadow Mountain Club.

I looked at Mother so happy and smiling and nodding. She's *always* that way, taking total pleasure in her Danny Boy—always the same, always, a kind of perpetual—oh, ecstasy, there's no other word for it, her whole life celebrating her first-born —

So I took it. Goddamn it, Danny Boy took the money again!

But there was something wrong with Mom. She'd be her perfect, beautiful self, as always, and then suddenly without warning she'd *flush*, she'd get all red like a bad sun-burn, and she'd perspire like crazy, Mom who always hated sweat. She'd get dizzy and lose her balance. I asked Dad what was the matter, but he didn't want to talk about it. I asked David too, and he just shrugged his shoulders and said, "I guess menopause is no picnic."

Mom and Dad decided to go see a doctor up at Loma Linda Hospital for some relief of Mom's symptoms; afterward they were going to Redlands for an alumni shindig at the U. of R. and a couple of days with Gram and Gramps. David and I were charged with holding the fort. We went to see *Psycho* at the Sun-Air Drive-In;

sitting out there in folding chairs beside the Coral Cad, we watched in growing fascination and terror. At the end my little brother and I were so scared, completely taken in—we had no idea Norman Bates was really his dead Mother. At midnight in the isolation of the empty White House, listening to the mournful coyotes out on the desert, David and I crept from room to room, turning on the lights.

The next evening David joined me at the table while I sipped my iced tea. When the family would sit around after one of Mom's big hearty dinners—she still insisted on making a feast, despite her fragile health—nobody would say anything about Danny's iced tea being a tall glass of bourbon and water. Nothing had changed, we all still believed in our willful refusal to acknowledge problems.

But now David wanted to figure things out, and he asked again about the whole speech contest business. I was pretty negative. David said he didn't understand; I was giving all those sermons, two-a-Sunday, and I was a hit with the Coachella Valley farmers—if I thought public speaking was so bad, why was I still doing it?

"Old habits die hard," I said.

He seemed confused.

David just looked at me as I poured myself some more "iced tea." Just the two of us, together, in The White House. Brothers. I said, "Look, man, you're an Eagle Scout. I was a Tenderfoot for three years, I cried on camp-outs. You're a Cowboy—I'm a devout sissy."

He grinned.

"If you go into speech contests, you won't be competing against other kids—you'll be competing against me."

He looked away again. "Well, I'm used to that."

Oh, shit.

I'm sorry.

Shit man, I'm really sorry.

"Don't do it," I said. "You can't win. I was up there on stage all the time. I didn't have any spare moments for little things. Like friends." I told him about the kids at Roosevelt Junior High in Eugene laughing at my salutation, "Fellow students…" I told him how the kids at Modesto High *groaned*. I gave him a whole string of examples.

"Wasn't there anything good about it at all?" he asked.

I took him into the hall and turned on the lights in my big trophy case. "Look at all that," I said. "Look at it. Do you realize how hard that was on me?"

David stared at the golden glow of the trophies. In his younger days, nobody liked to look at my trophy case more than David; he'd sit there, gazing, hypnotized.

He said, "If it was hard on *you*, think of all the kids who lost."

He had me there.

David paused, then asked, "If you had to do it all over again—would you?"

Oh, shit—well—of course I'd do it all over again, of course I would.

Right?

He said, "You don't know what it's like—you're a tough act to follow."

I asked David if he'd thought at all about what he wanted to be when he grew up. He said he'd really like to be a forest ranger. But he said maybe a forest ranger wasn't good enough for a member of the McCall family.

Oh, shit. Again.

The phone rang, Mother and Dad called to say they'd be home after supper.

"They're worried about your drinking," David said. "You hardly bother to hide it from them."

I shrugged it off. "No big deal."

"Maybe," he said.

We went out into the hot air of the desert night. David led me down to the corral and gave some oats or whatever to Apollo, speaking softly to her. And then he reached back behind one of the hay bales, where he'd hidden them—a pint of Early Times and a pack of Marlboros.

Jesus David! At least I waited until I was in college to break the bargain. But here you are, only fourteen —

David said, "I don't want to talk about it."

Suddenly he didn't look like my kid brother Eagle Scout anymore; he looked like one tough hombre. He took a drag at his cigarette, and a swig at the bottle, and then turned with his sad stone face and offered them to me. Hell, who am I to judge. Not being a hypocrite, I took them both.

As we stood there in the moonlight leaning over the fence, smoking and drinking, David muttered, "My merit badges for alcohol and tobacco."

The booze hit me pretty fast, I was still feeling the effects of my evening binge. We sat there on the fence. We both finished off our cigs and had another swig. Then he reached into his pocket, pulled out his pack of Marlboros, and offered me another one. Again he gave me that "don't give me any shit about it" look. We stood there leaning on the fence and smoking, staring at the beautiful desert moon. I looked at my brother, The Eagle Scout Chain Smoker Alcoholic. Maybe he *will* end up an alcoholic—I'm already headed that way.

Oh, David, I'm sorry, I've been a lousy big brother.

When Mother and Dad came home, I was still so drunk I didn't know if I could hide it. David escaped to go care for Apollo. I stood there and tried to be OK, but they could see it in my eyes. Danny, their darling *wunderkind*, shit-faced.

President Roy, deliberately non-comprehending as usual, retreated to his study to prepare for the upcoming faculty meeting. Mother took charge of the roast lamb and summer squash.

Afterward, she joined me in the living room on her apricot settee. As Mom and I sat alone together, I could see that the California Mother of the Year looked weak and terribly tired. She was still brooding over the Speech Contest business. She was very slow, chewing on her lip and shaking her head, she seemed—medicated somehow, suffering, in both physical and emotional distress. We kept our voices low.

Mother reminded me of glorious moments, treasures of a lifetime. She said, "You were so *good* at it, Danny. Your Dad and I talked about it—we thought you were enjoying it all."

"Mom, of course I did. Just this evening, when David asked me if I'd do it all over again, I said sure—*sure* I would."

That cheered her up. A faint little smile.

She sat there, trying to get things straight in her mind. "We didn't *push* you. You seemed to be having a grand time."

"I was. I *was*. But it kind of …backed up on me, I buried the strain, the confusion —"

And I thought, oh, Jesus, I was afraid this day would come, please let's not go through this —

I wanted to change the subject, staring at the tomato juice coagulating like blood at the bottom of my glass. But I couldn't get her to let go.

"Oh Danny, you don't *regret* those golden years?"

Mother, just let me get away from here and clear my head. Am I becoming an alcoholic, a boozy footnote to my adolescent glory? I'm so fucking angry, please leave me alone—

She was looking at me beseechingly. "Danny, we love you so, we *adore* you—"

And then she was in trouble—flushed, perspiring. She sat there, unsteady, waiting. She arose, took a step, faltered, and I grabbed her before she could fall, I took her in my arms, she was light as a feather, so frail, and I started to carry her into the bedroom—

Dad was there. In the hallway. Had he been eavesdropping? My father watched, sternly disapproving, his eyes big buckets of disappointment, as I drunkenly swaggered to the bedroom with his wife in my arms. I took Mother into the master bedroom, she was crying now, and I gently put her down on their king size bed.

I went back out into the hallway and shut the bedroom door, and there was Dad. He glared at me and made a fist, and Jesus, he slugged me in the jaw.

I was going to go into my own bedroom, I couldn't

figure out what to do or where to go, I stumbled into the bathroom for a minute, shaking my head, and then I saw Dad slumped in the old green rocking chair, his face in his hands. Tentatively I sat on the couch next to him, not knowing what the hell I could say.

"I was so afraid you'd drop her," he said.

I waited. Lamely I said, "Well, you've got a fine right cross for a man your age."

He sat there not saying anything.

Looking at him I admitted, "I shouldn't drink in front of my parents."

He said, slowly, "You shouldn't drink. Period. I've lost two brothers to Demon Rum. Rex strangled to death on his own vomit. Martin's gone, too, he slowly drifted away from us in a fog of alcohol. And now your mother's brother spends half his time drunk and the other half in rehabilitation. You've got it coming down on you from both sides." Roy C. McCall looked up at me with real tenderness, chastened by a command, "Be *careful*."

We both just sat there for a while in the silent dark of the living room.

Jesus, Charley Moyle was right, my whole family is a fucked-up Eugene O'Neill tragedy. And David—watch out, we've got it coming down on us from both sides. Shit, maybe David will end up a drug addict in the gutter someday.

I don't want to take that damn trip to London and Calcutta anymore—hell, I don't even want to go to Columbia. Maybe I should stay here. With my family.

Dad's face was ashen. He said, "Son, I'll carry that punch to my grave."

CHAPTER ELEVEN

THE FAR SIDE OF THE WORLD

"Were this world an endless plain, and by sailing eastward we could for ever reach new distances, and discover sights more sweet and strange than any Cyclades or Islands of King Solomon, then there were promise in the voyage. But in pursuit of those far mysteries we dream of, or in tormented chase of that demon phantom that, some time or other, swims before all human hearts while chasing such over this round globe, they either lead us on in barren mazes or midway leave us whelmed."

— Herman Melville, *Moby-Dick*

PART ONE
It's All Downhill from Here

Summer, 1961

My parents were excited for my "adventure overseas," and they reassured me that Mother was feeling better. As I pulled out to head for the airport, Dad waved to me and said, "Drive carefully—my son's in that car!"

I had read about my London hotel in *Europe on Five Dollars a Day*. It was a huge room with two double beds and a fake fireplace. Up on Tottenham Court Road I rented an enormous ancient typewriter and dragged it home through the Tube to Bayswater. I'd write in the morning from eight to twelve, like Thomas Mann, and then I had the rest of the day free for museums and movies and theatre.

Oh, a strange balance of foolishness and courage, humor and seriousness, I sat in my hotel room making notes. Since all my identity crises went right by me, I'd write my book about the years when Danny McCall, Native Son of the Golden West, was drowning in two inches of water. Speaking I did so well; I was *efficient*. Now I'm not. Not anymore, not at all—just writing, floundering. I have no clear goal, no prize to work for. Somewhere across the seas my great book was waiting for me. Politics and adventure, the great world, material—but in London I was far from the truth and I watched my pen give out. At night I dreamed about the trip to Sonoma where I had first heard the Legend of

Johnny Appleseed, where I had taken it down on tape, a sunny morning of hope.

In honor of the 4th of July I went and had a real American breakfast, scrambled eggs and bacon and toast, and as I sat there, drunk, I grabbed the International *Herald Tribune*. To my horror I read that Ernest Hemingway had taken his life in Ketchum, Idaho. NO! Grace Under Pressure? I couldn't believe it. I wandered for hours. Oh, it *can't* be so. Not Papa. At the library I re-read my old favorites, "Indian Camp," "The Killers," "Soldier's Home." I couldn't stop crying.

Man oh man, I was drinking a lot.

On Sunday I went to Speaker's Corner in Hyde Park. I couldn't stay away. A skinny fanatic about my age was preaching the Gospel from a little box, like Billy Graham. He had a shabby suit, crystal eyes, and a cloth sign: YOU ARE IMPORTANT. He couldn't attract a crowd, so I let him preach just to me.

Twenty feet away, a fat woman in a pink dress waved a red parasol and sang "Michael Row Your Boat Ashore" while a pudgy dwarf heckled her with jokes, a perfect comedy team. Perched on a little ladder behind the sign "Coloured Workers Welfare Association of Gt. Britain and Ireland," an old black man had no fingers on one hand and a glove on the other. His half-hand cracked like a mallet against the top of the wooden sign; he shouted, "I got 29 wives because I got the technique and I got the banana!" He was holding his own with the hecklers until a bald white man started up some competition. Stripped to the waist, the white man was scrawled all over with tattoos; his raw back looked like a lavatory wall in art school, while in front his nipples were the noses of two clowns. To the black orator he sneered, "Go back to Abyssinia," which spurred the reply, "Kiss my black arse." The tattooed man held up a large photograph of a gorilla: "Here's your father!" The crowd was really into it now. The old Negro banged his fingerless hand and the glove flew off the other one—revealing no hand at all—and he screamed, "Fuck off, you second-hand Anglo-Saxon!" He was spitting and foaming, "Next case! Next case!"

The white man held the photograph higher, waving it at the black man's head, shouting to the crowd, "Which one's the monkey?" In the background I could hear the vaudeville duo of the fat woman and the dwarf braying "You Are My Sunshine." On his high ladder the black man with his enormously expressive eyes cried out, "You call *us* savages? Are we the ones who use poison gas and kill Negroes like dogs in Mississippi? You call yourselves the Leaders of the Free World. You stink! You are corrupt! *You* are the savages!" Several American tourists were in the crowd, and they shouted up toward him towering on his ladder. One American girl protested, "No, no, it's not true." The black man displayed his white teeth: "One American at a time. You're not in Alabama now." He bent way forward, jackknifed over his sign, and hissed, "One at a time, you goddamned refugees in skyscrapers!"

It was a mad speech contest, TV Diablo gone berserk, a freak show. From somewhere back in the crowd there arose a pure clean note, it warbled, and broke into the hoot of a ghostly owl in the forest night. The hoot floated again, witchingly. I'm doing it, I'm really doing it, oh my God—people were moving back, creating room. Ladies and Gentlemen, let me tell you a story that is instructive and uplifting, Ralph Waldo Emerson himself said long ago he saw his job in life was twofold, to explain and to inspire—I wasn't sure whether I was speaking aloud or just thinking—

I scanned the crowd for eye contact, and on my left an American woman in her fifties, standing beside her husband in Bermuda shorts, was snapping my picture.

On my last day in London I was in the basement of the American Express office when I heard a voice from behind me and across the room: "Guess who's here?—Danny McCall."

I turned, half expecting a joke of some kind, when I saw a group of four boys about my age I didn't recognize. They weren't looking at me, they were gathered around a big black registry book where Americans sign in. The short one said, "Who?" and the tallest one pointed at my signature, saying, "Don't you remember? Danny McCall."

I strode over to them. "Hello."

The tall one, who had said my name, looked at me, puzzled; and then with a spasm of recognition said, "Danny McCall! It is you!" He shook my hand.

I was scanning their faces, I still didn't know them, and then suddenly I knew—from way back at Roosevelt Junior High in Eugene, the guy who remembered me, he was—what was his name?—Gary, yes, Gary, he was one of us in the first round of the Optimist Contest.

We repaired to a Piccadilly pub. The four of them had just graduated from the University of Oregon, and we exchanged frat stories. I kept picturing Gary as he was back in Junior High, I could see him in his big Strad shirts, purple ones, like me, he'd gotten his height when I hadn't yet.

The Piccadilly pub closed for the afternoon recess. Out on the sidewalk Gary said, "When you went on to high school, did you do anymore public speaking?"

"No, no," I lied, waving my hand as if that was kid stuff.

But Gary's eyes were fixed on a memory. "Remember how we practiced in front of each other in the Roosevelt cafeteria?" He continued, smiling slyly, mocking me: "Six Navy fliers who drowned in a raging sea —"

Gary paused, lost in thought. Then he leaned in, and whispered, "How does it feel Danny—knowing it's all downhill from here?"

Back at the hotel I lay on my bed and finished my bottle of gin. I couldn't stop thinking about it—"How does it feel, knowing it's all downhill from here?"— it was so dreadful, it's not, it's NOT, thepastisprologue! How dare he say such a cutting and unkind and foolish thing to me?

I seemed to be talking to myself out in Left Field. Why didn't I go into theatre at Stanford? Why didn't I continue speaking and performing? Then I'd be ready to do something grand, not squander my time in London holed up in a hotel room getting dead drunk and writing. In the Waterville paper, in all those California papers, it said I was planning a career in TV and the stage. What happened to that career, where did I go wrong? I mean, okay, so even if it's all downhill from here, Danny, you don't have to *schuss* it!

I had read once that "Byzantine art is an escape from the personal." I want to escape *into* the personal. But it's hard to do that in America, especially after the music. I'd know how to escape into the personal if—if—if I were sure I wanted to, if I thought I could do it without escaping into the negligible. I know I have a very feeble sense of the irrevocable, I know I make conceits instead of connections. But it is so hard in America to test your will and character, to find yourself, without falling back on some conventional image of success.

What's the matter with you, Champ?

Mother always said I looked like, spoke like, Billy Graham. Who do I look like now? I went into the bathroom and stared at myself in the mirror. I gazed past myself to the reflection of the toilet and the red drapes, I searched beyond to where all the people were, the thousands in the Crystal Ballroom, I whispered to the multitudes in my eyes in my face in the mirror:

> LOVE MY ASS, YOU FUCKERS, I AM
> WHAT YOU BELIEVE IN

For seventeen years my mother and father had convinced me that I was the center of the universe. And my career didn't provide much evidence to the contrary.

No—truly, I shouldn't have majored in theatre at Stanford. I was one shrewd freshman, I saw it immediately, knew my business was to get it on the page. What a movie my story could make, my reputation in America would be assured. I could go on speaking tours and plug the book, return to *Today* for a chat with Dave Garroway. The Return of Dangerous Schizophrenic.

Dangerous Schizophrenic Strikes Again. I would beat my past, cheat it of its due, Lions-Optimist-American-Legion-Native-Son—the book would prove I *wasn't* better at 17 than at 21. I had grown. I had continued, cultivated my gifts. After all the hoop-la over the book, I'd make a provision in the contract for the film sale: I had to have a part in the movie. Then I'd get my career rolling again, and move on to politics. I know why I majored in English. To write this book. The book *has* to be good, I smiled.

But could I tell about my parents? Looking up at the ceiling I asked myself, what's my earliest memory of them? Finally I had it. I could remember when I was three years old, lying in my bed, listening to Mother sing "Danny Boy," the song I was named for. As I drifted into sleep the pipes, the pipes were calling for me, Mother's perfect voice lifted slowly and softly up to where the hills were waiting, with trailing cascades of devotion: oh Danny boy, oh Danny boy, I love you so.

I glanced at my cheerful note from Mother and Dad, with "worlds of love" to their "wonderful son so far from home." I never told my parents that they gave me the answers on *Strike It Rich*. Should I tell them now? Before I die? Or do they already know?

At the end of the hall sat an old ball-and-claw footed tub. I took a bath in the cold water, eyes shut tight.

PART TWO
Calcutta

Summer, 1961

Calcutta was misery, endless misery. For an hour, sweating stains into my clothes, my ass bleeding, I sat in the airlines bus hating, blindly hating. The Indian girl in uniform let me off at the corner, where she said I could live for $35 a week. The heavy sky was lying close to the city like an army blanket. Humidity: 94. Temperature: 109. No Americans in sight. I pulled my bag off the bus and trudged up the brick path to the hotel where snakes lived in monstrous trees. Signing in, I stared at the water on the backs of my hands. Gray storm light, air like soup, I was an American. Through a little window I saw a snake writhe down a limb and disappear into tall grass behind a sacred cow, asleep.

My room was confined and intolerable, like the room in Louisville. I locked the door from the inside. I watched the old rickety fan in the ceiling, turned it to top speed where the machine-rattle sounded like applause. I stood there and gave my Optimist Speech, word for word, timing it, finishing with Fosdick's fidelity at 4:43. I tottered. I was coming down with something; my neck was all cramped up, I couldn't turn my head sideways. If I wanted to see something over there, I had to turn my whole body. As I paced under the crippled fan, I felt ill, quite ill.

In fitful sleep I had nightmares like those I had always had when the Judges were compiling their scores and comparing their ballots. False. I always won. I knew I shouldn't be so hard on myself. Don't wallow in pointless pain, they'll announce it in a minute and then you can coast home on that great unicycle in the sky.

In the morning the fever was back, I was still sweating and shitting blood. Hungover and ill, I blundered through alleys looking for a crowd of Indians to address. Indians, come here, I will speak wise sentences to you. Indians, *look* at me! If I run down the street, as fast as I can, they'll look. Panting in the middle of an empty intersection, I'll draw myself up, Speaker Number One. I can show a clot of urchins how to clap, they can just sit around me and applaud for five minutes, and I'll give them something. Then I can go to the zoo and watch the peacocks shriek.

Tramping in the Calcutta streets, I was suddenly whirled back, stopped dead by a long piece of tin, a reflection: there I was, licking cholera-Scotch air, wearing dark glasses, caught in the mirror of a tailor's shop. So what if all the dummies in the store window had dust all over them, I went inside. The tailor was middle-aged, spoke English, rather quiet and gentle, bemused, so I did it—I was treated royally as I stood still to be measured for my British double-breasted white linen suit. We had tea, and I could pick it up the next day, there was a slow time, he had his boys ready. I paid him with a traveler's cheque. The bossman wanted me to come see his garden, his best boy had heard of the University of Stanford. When I returned next evening, my white suit was ready: I preened, I loved myself, home at last, and checked it out in that tin mirror where I had been so frightened.

On my way back to the hotel it began to rain in

the trees full of snakes. Where is that Northern doctor, the one who waved his umbrella in the heavy air of the Crystal Ballroom, I probably just need the proper medication—

I came to a huge public park glistening in gray light. I trudged. The park went on forever, and in muddy pools children were sloshing around naked and happy and doomed. Whole families urinating and cooking. The people were miserable and didn't know I existed; if they glanced at me they just looked through me and went on about their suffering.

I never looked at people, people looked at me. But these Indians *can't see me*. Guess who's not here?— Danny Mc… Dann…Da –

In my hotel room I dried myself off and picked up the newspaper. Every day a hundred people were taken to the hospital with cholera, there was a little bold-face cholera-box on the front page, like a weather report.

Life is cheap.

"Exterminate all the brutes!" That's it, I'm Kurtzing out, I just got fascinated with *Heart of Darkness*, got spellbound with Masterpieces of Modern Literature. Sure I remember Marlow's Kurtz, "vibrating with eloquence," the man who "electrified large meetings"— that's it. I want "magnificent eloquence thrown to me from a soul as translucently pure as a cliff of crystal," I hunger for "unspeakable rites" because I got a dose of Romantic Agony, I'm one of T.S. Eliot's Hollow Men—

Mistah Appleseed—he dead
      A trophy for the Old Guy[5]

---

5 The opening lines of T.S. Eliot's poem "The Hollow Men":
Mistah Kurtz—he dead / A penny for the Old Guy

College isn't where you learn anything, it's just the place where you put everything you know upside down, and then you congratulate yourself for standing on your head—

When I get back to the real world I'll probably regain fifteen pounds, and then this white suit won't even be wearable, it'll just remind me of this blotto ugliness where even my legitimate physical and mental disorder was BOOKS —

So tell your life story. All you need is a title!

I Was Johnny Appleseed for the FBI
From Appleseed to Asshole
The Sore Winner
Johnny Fucking Appleseed

Johnny Appleseed in *Calcutta*? You've got to be kidding.

How can I use written words to kill spoken words? If I can't live it down, must I write it down?

More Scotch!

When I woke up I put my fingers to my head and I could still feel the buzz. I prowled among sacred cows, dying beggars, and starving children. That night, drunk and weaving my way back in the dark to the entrance of the Snake Tree Hotel, playing leap-cow, the purple Indian woman suddenly noticed me. Since I'm in my brand new double-breasted white suit (who is this yo-yo dressed like Mark Twain?), she came over to me, with dagger eyes, and aching all over I said "yes"—

And with but the most meagre of preliminaries she accepted my money and laid it on the table. On the hotel bed the purple Indian woman pushed my shoulders back, put my arms behind my head, and inserted me into her living body for my money, and she began to do it, this woman with her sad sinister grin, this is what it all comes down to, this bargain, sex is something you *buy*—

I was pumping, pumping, hoping for the best, and her face became several faces, she's turning into some Hindu demon, no, no, it's the Scotch, she's just a thin corrupt woman, this prostitute of the great sub-continent, riding me, bored—does she know I'm an alcoholic?—no I can't win this one, she seems disappointed, not like Sondra, the prostitute who had been so gentle with me—

And right in the middle, just comin' down the backstretch, an older woman with gray hair came through the door, just walked right in with a mop and a bucket, and she merely glanced at us, two human beings in the most intimate relationship God ever thought up, and the old woman spilled the bucket on the dusty floor and began to mop. And the prostitute, this lady who only noticed me when I was in my double-breasted white suit, this lady who now is, she's—she's *picking* her *nose*!—her purple finger explored her purple nostril as she barked instructions—

The two women were talking in beetle-juice language, the old woman was slopping efficiently in the corners of the room, jabbering away in Hindi-Jeebee, those two women were arguing with each other, and I suppose it's funny, but it's not funny anymore, not at all, did I—

Did I swallow the marble or just say I did?

"*Get outta here!*" I finally yell out, and the older woman leaves, and the woman on top is looking at me with her eyebrow that says when *will* you finish?, and me, dear me, pumping for all I'm worth—

The golden bed came down from the sky as they humped up to heaven together, a little man and a hooker clad in, well, whatever she had just cast aside—

> *And Kurtz's last words were*
> *E - liz - a - beth Black -well*

The next morning I awoke on the floor. It seemed that I had been passed out there for some time. I was dressed again, in my wet white suit.

In the matter of sex I was the last to know. In everything else I was the first. I was a kid who believed in America and God and pleasing his parents and giving sermons disguised as orations and orations disguised as sermons.

Now, in the hell of Calcutta, I wondered if I was dying.

Wandering in bazaars, fending off beggars, I saw a vendor's cardboard box full of knives. I thought David the Eagle Scout might like a knife, so I bought one, a green switch-blade. I turned the knife over and over in my pocket.

Back in my hotel room I thought of calling home. Hearing the voices of the folks, on the other side of the world—yes, that would calm me down. But when I had tried to call them from the airport we had a bad connection, and I kept shouting into the phone, "What—say something—I can't hear you—*what?*" And they must have thought I was crazy.

I went to my desk and poured another glass of scotch. I snapped open the green switchblade. It felt greasy and I knew it was lethal. I wondered if the police could ever catch me. Could the local cops trace one of their dead Indians to the Boy of the Year? Where is the motive? If I didn't kill a human being, I could at least cut a cow's hump, plunge into it and run like mad as it awakened and roared and struggled from its rickety slept-on legs.

I tore a piece of paper into slips, signed each one, and gathered them up neatly on my desk. I bothered the pile of signatures delicately with the knife. The kind of energy that went into "the power to thrill and impress" was all mixed up with green knives and white suits—not the *first* fucked up white suit, *this* fucked-up one—and any story we want can justify our dim sense of primal trauma. That's it, let's blame it all on the bargain with grandfather—my primal trauma was just *Let's Make a Deal* —

I could just shut up about it, but I can't leave it alone because I don't want mirrors to scare me all the time—

And here I am in India where I don't want to speculate on the sound of one hand clapping, I want to recapture the sound of a thousand hands clapping—

I observed the green switchblade and handed it to me.

It's this knife, bunkum artist. This very knife.

Do it! Do it now. You have this slimy switch-blade to plunge into your Dangerous Schizophrenic's heart—hoist on your own *boutade*, man —

Listen, you may never have a chance like this again, so you better take it. The only way you are going to write that book is to kill its ostensible subject.

Someone was watching me. I felt it. Somebody

was looking at me, wanting me. My eyes toyed with the knife. I'll kill him if he tries anything.

I turned naturally from my desk and waited. Calmly, I peered into corners. Is there something you wish to say? I held my disciplined body in my trim white suit.

Definitely. Someone's watching me.

But who is he?

What if I turn around and he's a crowd?

What if I turn around and he's me?

I spun with the knife, a surprise attack—backing into a corner, blade out—come on, come and get it—

The voice whispered: "Kill yourself, not an Indian. Kill Danny McCall."

"The hell I will," I cried out. "NOBODY KILLS DANNY MCCALL, NOT EVEN ME!"

CHAPTER TWELVE

L'ENVOI

"I wish I was Cary Grant."
— Cary Grant

"In this country where everything is done to prove life isn't tragic, they feel something is missing… One must reject the tragic after having looked at it, not before."
— Albert Camus, *American Journals*

October 1962, New York City

But Calcutta didn't kill me.

And I managed to lock away the memories of my nightmare.

By the fall of 1962, I'd used my Danforth fellowship to complete the first year of graduate school in English at Columbia. I decided to write a letter to the Duchess; I briefly summarized the year after Stanford, and wrote that "something had happened to me in Calcutta that I wanted to talk with her about." But how could I ever explain? Was I just drunk out of my mind? Delirious from the fever? Letting loose my demons so I could write?

Her answering letter was astonishing. There was lots of the old funny stuff. She was presiding over the "slush pile" at the unsolicited manuscripts department of a publishing firm; she'd "just read a cowboy novel by an *autodidact* from Wyoming," and the sheriff's name was Carson McCullers. There was also a long paragraph about our old graduate-student-teacher-cronies, the bad ones making a name for themselves and the good ones being let go. She wondered if I was "death-driven," and said I should stop pretending I was a character in my own novel. She wished me well, hoped to see me again someday, and noticed how nostalgic she suddenly found herself that morning.

But I never did see the Duchess again, or tell her about my Calcutta nightmare; she married and moved overseas, and we fell out of touch. It felt like I had somehow lost my sister. I was relieved by her last letter—we weren't sordid and she wasn't bitter.

I knew I had to have her. Miss Kaufmann. My French teacher at Columbia. She was extraordinary—too challenging to be merely "different"; she spoke and moved like no one I'd ever known. She was knowledgeable, undeceived, and at the same time so ready to believe in you. It was the—the *combination*. Like for a lock. Walking up and down Riverside Drive I looked up at the single tower of Harry Emerson Fosdick's church and promised my fidelity to Miss Kaufmann as true as though she were already mine.

She was a grad student too, writing her Ph.D. thesis on the existential theatre of Jean-Paul Sartre. Our class met faithfully, a dozen of us, for an hour and a half Tuesday and Thursday evenings; Miss Kaufmann was teaching us enough French to pass the language requirement. I loved the way her ass moved when she erased the blackboard. She liked my big floppy blue overcoat—it was ten years old, Dad's coat from Eugene, and it came down to my shins. "Someday, Mr. McCall, that coat will fly away with you."

I wanted to ask her for a date, but it was awkward, teacher-student.

I decided to write her a sonnet; it would fit, a language requirement. I had to fabricate a seduction piece. I labored through the week but hadn't intended for it to be quite that hard to come by: the fourteen lines kept wandering all over. After days of cross-eyed satisfaction with iambic pentameter at two a.m. and gaping dejection in the clear light of morning, I sat in her evening class at Hamilton Hall. Under her steady gaze, all I could do was play with my second quatrain on the margin of my notebook. I did, however, ace the quiz. When class was over I grabbed my books, nodded to her and marched down the three flights of stairs to my post in the lobby. Before leaving my apartment I had put two glasses of sherry into the refrigerator and tucked the sonnet into my desk drawer.

For five minutes she did not come down. I gobbled water from the fountain; I paced back and forth. When I heard the familiar click of her heels, I went to the stone steps. Outrage! She was with swarthy Mr. Gold, the social scientist in the front row. I thought she looked vaguely dismayed as she went by. I nodded—Not Waiting For You, Not At All, Not Crushed—letting the two of them go past. I hoped they might part at the corner. Oh, please let them part at the corner. I followed at a safe distance, a prowler, until they disappeared together into the sidewalk crowd. I stood there at Broadway and 116th Street, looking up and down. Just when I had decided to give up, a ratty blast turned me around, and I saw them: my French Teacher went flying by on the back of Mr. Gold's motorcycle.

When I opened the refrigerator door, I found those two glasses of frosted sherry, those twin cups of gold, those seduction devices. I drank them both, double hemlocks, and stared out across the dark Hudson River to the lights on the Jersey Palisades. And then drank some more.

I loved my little apartment on the 12th floor. I'd got it on a sub-let from a jazz trumpeter; once a week he'd come back from his tour, collect his mail, and stand in the bathroom practicing so as not to lose his lip. There were lots of Stanford kids in New York and big parties down on 88th Street and over on Amsterdam. We had come to the big city to affront our destinies.

After class on Thursday night I beat Mr. Gold to her. I maneuvered her out to the brick courtyard. We were approaching the corner, and if she made it to Broadway I was afraid I wouldn't be able to turn her around. So in my father's blue overcoat I stopped in my tracks and I said to her, "I've been working on a poem with some French phrases in it. Could you take a few minutes to give me some help? I live just down the street here." If I hesitated, I'd lose it. I took a step toward Riverside Drive and made my eyes do an inquisitive trick. I moved so quickly that she was off-guard.

She said ok.

The rest of the way, four eyes watched four feet. At my apartment building I held the elevator door open for her, and we rode up twelve stories in neutral corners. She held her books across her boobs. My apartment was neat as a pin; the sherry was cooling its golden heels in the fridge. The sonnet, full-ready and blossoming, lay in the desk drawer. I had left on the lamp beside the bed.

She looked around and said, "Mr. McCall, you live in a cookie-box."

I took her coat. While I was hanging it in the closet she moved to the big front windows, circled the cookie-box and then sank onto the plum sofa. I produced the frosted glasses of sherry, drank mine much too quickly, and poured myself another. I stepped over to the window and stared at Grant's tomb. I wanted to bring out the sonnet—she was ripe, so ripe— but I held off. Her brilliant blue eyes so full of light were scary.

She said, "What brings you to Columbia?"

Well, I confessed I was a Danforth Fellow.

She frowned. "Isn't that religious?"

I tried to indicate that I didn't take it seriously. Not in these dark days of bargain-basement Pantheism.

With her second drink she relaxed and slipped one shoe off and tucked her leg up under her on the sofa. Her legs had lovely freckles. We conversed about French, France, and California. I was being extremely dull; I began to hope that I was being intentionally dull. I was The Lame Duck Amendment.

Finally she said, "You wanted help with a poem?"

I grabbed for a Marlboro and pulled my chair up to the desk. I said, "Just remember as I read it, it's *so* outrageous that it's all right."

She nodded. "Cocteau says the artist has to know how far to go too far."

What?

"Right," I said.

"Can't I read it myself?"

"No—oh, no I gotta read it to you."

She smiled, a little nervous. "Okay."

"But remember—it's *sufficiently* outrageous."

She smiled again, slightly annoyed. "I'll try to remember."

I braced myself and took out the piece of paper on which I had typed it. "More sherry?"

She fluttered her hand negatively over her glass.

There was no way out. I sighed. I said, "My poem is called 'To His French Teacher.'"

"Oh!"

She said that—perfectly—Miss Kaufmann said,

"Oh!"

"And I have a phrase in the first stanza here—*de cap a pie*. That means 'from head to toe.' In Old French."

"I know."

"Oh—right." Of course you do, you're the teacher. Then—well, I just read the whole thing to her, slowly, my voice groping for the tone and rhythms of a bed-directed rake:

TO HIS FRENCH TEACHER

> I'll never learn the language under you
> In academic gown *de cap a pie,*
> So I suggest that you come under me
> Where I can spend myself translating you.
> I know a proper mistress ought to take
> Especial care with students on the make;
> Like adjectives around a noun they cling,
> All set upon your person, place, or thing.
> But I propose only a seminar
> To teach you, teacher, sense to educate;
> The verb we study is quite regular,
> Employed by everyone to conjugate.
> > *Allons*! Our conversation will redeem
> > All learned intercourse in Academe.

There.

I studied the page. Now I'd done it.

I looked up: her bright blue eyes were staring straight ahead into the lamplight. She took a long pull on her sherry. I started to say something, caught myself, and handed the paper to her. I sat in silence while she read it and sipped her sherry. She let the shoe fall off her other foot and drew that other leg up under her. Now neither leg's lonely.

At last she said, "I should write you a poem back."

"Oh— No Backs." I stood up and walked toward her. Did I really say 'No Backs?'

She looked at me.

The sonnet had worked—and it hadn't.

"Well," I said—oh, for Chrissakes—"I, uh, I guess I should take you home."

I managed to bundle her into her coat and get her down the elevator and into my stupid blue Ford. My MG—where's my MG?

We sat so far away from each other.

I went uptown past Riverside Church and then doubled back onto Broadway. She gave me directions, and we drove a few blocks past Columbia down West End Avenue to 107th, I parked in the only available space near a yellow fireplug. I couldn't blow it now. I didn't try to kiss her; I stared at her and opened the door. I made it around the rump of my Ford; she got out and we crossed the street. We stood uncommitted in the entrance to her apartment house.

She's going to leave me here. After our sonnet. I'm A Dangerous Schizophrenic. New York's full of 'em.

She read the dismay in my eyes. "I owe you a cup of coffee."

My soul began to dance.

I held her books while she fumbled with her keys.

We walked up. And up. All the way, five flights, to the top. I was wheezing when we stopped at her black door. "Every day?" I said. "You do this every day?"

Unlocking the door she said, "I live clean."

Oh.

It was big and lovely, three dormer windows facing 107th. I sat in the nearest couch. There was a big Persian carpet in the center of the room.

I took off my shoes, and my teacher smiled.

She went into the kitchen to fix the coffee. While she was gone I spied the john, hopped in and peed sherry. Then I returned to all the roomy space in the old sighing furniture. She was standing at her desk under a print of an Etruscan flute player. I looked at her, walked over, put my arms around her and kissed her. She shuddered and opened to me.

Oh, my dear Miss Kaufmann—

I picked up my French Teacher and took her to the bed. Gently I laid her there. I sat down beside her, leaning over her, and we stared silently at each other.

She rolled herself out from under me, and headed for the bathroom.

I sat there and then pulled down the bedspread. A satin quilt was piled behind a chest of drawers; I put the quilt down carefully, patted it and laid it out at the foot of the bed. The headboard was walnut—it looked antique, the wood was dark and the craftsmanship fine. I took off all my clothes and laid them on a chair. Naked, I studied four photographs hung over the bed, a quartet of Paris street scenes—men fishing under a bridge in the Seine, night snow on a line of cars, nuns huddled in the wind against the grey of Notre Dame, children in a small park.

She sure was taking her time.

I strode, cold and naked around the room; I

investigated the Etruscan flute player's feet. On her desk was a dormant blue candle, half burned down and sitting there dead. When she still did not come out, I reached into my pants pocket for a matchbook, strolled naked back to the desk and lit the candle. I stood admiring my body in the glow. I grew tired of my body and started pacing.

In my solitary walk on the Persian carpet, it hit me: she's not getting ready for sex. She is simply sitting on the john. Something has disagreed with her. Me, probably. She will flush and re-enter this room, and I will be standing at her blue candle, a naked graduate student whose homework she has to grade.

I raced back into my clothes, put on and tied my shoes, went to the big front windows and sat, breathing hard. I gradually quieted down and pulled one leg up over the chair and watched garbage cans on 107th.

The toilet flushed. All around the closed bathroom door, like a stencil, the light snapped out, and my French Teacher emerged, supremely nude and delicate, out into the glow of the blue candle and me quite dressed, my shoe dangling over the arm of the chair.

"Oh"—she said, and stepped back out of the candlelight into shadow.

"I"—I said, "you took so long, I —"

I raced back out of my clothes and took her hand. Her body was unbearably rich: those freckles on her shoulders, the white of her breasts and sides and belly. She reclined on the quilted bed, I reclined over her.

O my America! My New-found-land!
Miss Kaufmann
Dorothy

One little room an everywhere—

We traded life stories. Her parents were refugees from Nazi Germany who got to New York in 1936; in the First World War, her father had fought in the German army at *Verdun*.

I listened. Amazing.

And then she asked me about me.

I started at the beginning. I told her the story of the Optimist Contest in Louisville, the Crystal Ballroom, all the winning. I told her about Harry Emerson Fosdick writing the letter to his future wife—I could feel my voice slipping into oratory and I didn't care—look, Miss Kaufmann, here's the country, I'll show you—Fosdick, the pastor of that Riverside Church we passed last night, Fosdick wrote that though they had not yet met, and he did not know who she was, he would keep his fidelity to her as true as though she were already his—

She said it sounded creepy.

CREEPY? It wasn't *creepy* in Louisville. What the hell do you mean?

She nodded. "Yes, creepy—a twelve-year-old boy talking about sexual fidelity to a thousand people."

"Listen, Dorothy, I was a *champion* public speaker. You should have heard me—I was beautiful—in Louisville, in Muskogee, in Waterville, on the *Today* show. And let me tell you something—I leaned down to her, my voice furiously soft—"I was the best." I let it sink in. "The *best*. Nobody could hold a crowd like Danny Boy. You want to know what I could do with people in the audience? I could wrap them around my little finger." I paused, distracted, "I've got a roomful of golden trophies, a *roomful*, and I really don't know, I don't know what to do with 'em now—"

She said, "You could have them melted down into a golden calf."

A Golden Calf?!

In mock anger I retorted, "Jesus, Dorothy, I'm from America, and you're just from Queens!"

She laughed, but then her smile faded. Her extraordinary blue eyes looked baffled. They turned cold. "When I was little my father read me the story of Pinocchio, and I remember being scared by the Island of Lost Boys. She looked at me. "Doesn't sound like you ever had a chance to be a Real Boy."

She was on to me. And she wanted truth.

She lay there thinking under the quilt. A little hazy she said, "If we had been in high school together, would I have liked you?"

I looked away again. Oh, be serious, Miss Kaufmann. You would have hated me—

or —

well—

I kept it from all the kids, I kept it a secret—

maybe you would have liked *Death of a Salesman*—

no, sorry, you wouldn't have liked me at all.

We sat facing each other like statues. She started to say something, then thought better of it.

I could feel Danny Boy sinking, slowly going under, a defunct Americanism Champ.

She looked me over skeptically and covered herself with the quilt. She seemed—betrayed, somehow. "Some men," she said, "can talk to a thousand people as if they're talking to one person."

"Yeah?"

"With you it's the other way around."

After our desultory goodbye I found myself sitting back in my apartment, alone with my thoughts.

Dark images of Calcutta invaded my brain.

I sat there. And sat there.

I'm gonna go live in Nebraska.

I walked the several blocks back to Miss Kaufmann's apartment, and climbed all the flights to her black door. I stood there in Dad's big blue coat and knocked and called in, "Poetry Man. Somebody's got to sign for this sonnet."

"Get lost!"

"I *am*."

I waited an eternity.

At last she came, in a pale blue robe.

It was extremely awkward, sitting there in silence at her little round table. I thought of several things to say, and they were all terrible. She was so threatening. Maybe I should just write it off as a good lay and laugh all the way back to my cookie-box. Golden fucking *calf*. But I looked at her carefully, she was utterly lovely, and I couldn't bear to leave. Goddamn that—*combination*.

The light in her room was chill and clear. She took her empty coffee cup to the sink.

"My story begins," I said quietly, "up in a little town they call Vermont."

She couldn't hear, the water was running.

"Folks never rightly knew John's last name, and they figured they'd call him after his trade—so they called him Johnny Appleseed."

She turned off the faucet, put the cup in the rack, and when she came out I put my arms around her, sat her down in the straight t chair by the table. The Guardeen Angel was Ev Dirksen—I leaned on the b.s. aspect of that angel, leaned a little harder than I had previously—but the spirit was intact. In her apartment on 107th Street, I was lost, Manhattan so hard and dirty—

"The settlers sang as they passed John's orchard,
'Get on the wagon rolling west,
Come on to the great unknown,
Get on the wagon rolling west,
Or you'll be left alone....
(faintly, in the distance)
Or you'll be left... *alone?*'

Get it? Dorothy?

Aw, *Chere Maitresse*, let me explain. Johnny Appleseed was always alone, that's the whole *point*. People didn't have anything to do with it. He crossed the continent alone; in some ways he was the only man on it.

And I could still do it. I had the pure feeling at the center of it; Johnny's voice was clearly fragile, and when he was planting, the owl hooted, the real owl. In front of Miss Kaufmann I hunched and popped into forest critters, the owls answering each other, the rabbits, the big ol' bear; then Johnny old and cranky at the end of his great journey, at the end of his long solitary life—

Dorothy, forgive me, it's not red and white and blue bullshit, it's a dream, you judge it by how beautiful it is, it's a legend, it's a myth, it's humor, it's a song—

Her face smoothed out into dismayed wonder. She sat at her little table with her dishtowel bunched in front of her.

Please understand, Miss Kaufmann: I have a great future behind me.

At the end I held it there for a moment, then relaxed, and sat with her at the table. I was lost looking at her.

Jesus, Dorothy, I'm only 22, I'm not over it yet, it'll take time to pull out of it, I got myself into it so *deep*, it really was so *taxing* to be the boy I was, I mean I'm sorry, and now I'm just all upset, nobody ever gives me a chance, that's why I fuck up-so bad, I'll try to get over all this Calcutta shit, I'm not a violent person, I'm just doing my best, like I've always done, so if you could please just help me —

> *Oh, Danny, nobody can tell you what you already know. In tight spots, when you're threatened, you will always go back to Johnny Appleseed. You will perpetually attempt to reproduce yourself there.*
>
> *And that means—Mr. Renner was right, I won't ever be mature. Just bitter. A bachelor, at three a.m. wandering drunk on the endless Great Plains, shouting Johnny Appleseed to the wind. Falling into wheat. Wondering whether it's worth it to get up. And I had so much—so much—*
>
> *Promise.*
>
> *Choose one: (A) If you're over it, have you lost it? (B) If you've lost it, are you over it? Enclose a winged figure with your answer.*
>
> *magic*
> *magic*

magic

I want to be a child again, with it all before me, where to choose.

You have been a perfect fool—and you are no longer perfect.

Sitting there at her table, she had me, she absolutely had me, the way she was looking at me.

It's *me* Dorothy, I'm *here* now, so don't hurt me, don't ruin it—

She studied my face. Finally she asked with a wary smile, "Who are you, anyway?"

AFTERWORD

O reader, do you understand this story I'm telling you, and why I am telling it this way and in this voice? What do you want, Irony?

Do you think that boy is someone this man is ashamed of?

I am trying to acquaint you with a syndrome.

This is not an autobiography; it is not to my purpose, and none of your business, to show the years between the whore-house and my writing now, my working here in this summer night, the smell of the humid darkness coming in my window, the sound of my darling son's sleeping, his quiet breathing—these very cadences have nothing to do with it.

It would be silly, if not terrifying, if I had to explain.

O, my reader, you have walked into my room. Please go away, for I have to trust you to know what I'm not doing here.

— Dan's handwritten note
found in 1986 draft

Boy on a Unicycle is Dan McCall's story told in Dan McCall's words. As editor, I allowed myself narrative license to consider every sentence he had written. Perhaps there are readers who wish this was a "found" manuscript, a complete and polished relic hidden away in his basement. Perhaps that would be a nice romantic story.

But in truth, my father left behind an overwhelming number of documents, tens of thousands of pages piled up loosely or stuffed into boxes, in the office and the basement and the guest room, papers everywhere crammed onto shelves between thousands of books. (In the last years of his life, his deteriorating eyesight contributed to the disarray). On the living room carpet I organized my archaeological dig site into dozens of stacks with color-coded labels such as *Memoir, Hemingway Research,* and *Epistolary Novel.*

I distilled memoir pages from four distinct periods: 1970, 1986, 1999, and 2006. Although he stubbornly resisted modern technology ("tools of the devil," he'd jest), in his later years Dan conceded to hiring a typist; separating out memoir pages printed via computer revealed the two slightly distinct versions from 1999 and 2006. In reconciling these later drafts, my goal was to choose passages where real emotion was not overshadowed by the glare of his talent. I imagined my father's voice quoting Ralph Waldo Emerson: "Cut these words and they would bleed; they are vascular and alive."

I then turned to a batch of papers with distinctly different typeface—older, yellower, and decayed with age. As I pieced together the original drafts from 1970, I found scenes discarded long ago which to my eyes seemed new. Dan had omitted dozens of pages chronicling his more ordinary high school experiences about participation in basketball and tennis, singing in the choir, and picking peaches in the summer. But on occasion I'd find a passage and think, "This is too good —I have to put it back in."

The 1970 versions had compelling immediacy and precise detail. For example, regarding his initial foray into public speaking, I chose for the final text his lengthier and more nuanced original paragraph with the lines "My voice surprised me, it was naked, it bounced over their heads from the pale green walls" and "my face was itching, everywhere, a fly crawling around on it." I also re-included one entire section: Frank Brasil's hayride, where the teenagers sneak away from the bonfire to go necking under the moonlight. Most importantly, I felt this scene served a vital function to further the needs of the plot. Seeing Danny try to live up to 'the bargain' (e.g., "I held the (wine) bottle up and pretended to take a big swig") boosts the payoff later on for the crazed drinking scene at Stanford.

In the versions written in his mid-forties, Dan expanded upon his harrowing ordeal in India. While compiling these last remaining drafts from 1986, with their distinctive print from his old Royal typewriter, I immediately hoped the Calcutta material could serve as the emotional anchor to his story. Dan laid bare his battle with inner demons; but in later versions, he discarded it. When I found a letter from his friend and colleague Kevin Murphy critiquing a later draft (without Calcutta), it confirmed the decision to embrace Dan's earlier instinct:

"…I thought this American story was leading to a

deep, bad fall that never happens. Not that you have to end up face-down in a swimming pool with a cluster of leaves tracing a red circle in the water. But you provide what seem so many anticipations of the personal and private inadequacy of the success you were groomed for that, without some reappraisal, agonizing or otherwise, you seem to be ducking the very issue you're trying to grapple with."

Calcutta is the "deep, bad fall" this painful story requires. In the end, I felt 'younger Dan' should overrule 'older Dan' and include this haunting chapter.

While editing *Boy on a Unicycle*, one main question drove me: "Where in hell did my father's *anger* come from?" After two years immersing myself in his memoir I can't say I fully understand it. But I'm close enough.

In his penetrating book about male depression, aptly titled *I Don't Want to Talk About It*, Terrance Real writes: "...boys don't hunger for fathers who will model traditional mores of masculinity. They hunger for fathers who will rescue them from it... Sons don't want their father's "balls"; they want their hearts. And, for many, the heart of a father is a difficult item to come by. Oftentimes, the lost boy the depressed son must recover is the one not he but his father has disavowed."

As the author's son, it was cathartic to understand his primal trauma from long ago. I could envision him as a wounded teenager, terrified of revealing vulnerability to his parents. In a scene where Danny confesses to a contest he'd actually *lost*, he added, "oh why don't they help me, why don't they love me just for myself, the little dope jerk I really am?"

Another pile of papers revealed a handwritten note condemning his parents:

Mom and Dad used me —they <u>used</u> me, for <u>their</u> ambition. God does not exist. There is no plan for the universe. I'm all trembling, I'm shot, I'm going to be nothing but an alcoholic. They used that fucking 'bargain' to beat me into submission.

Discovery of this heart-wrenching paragraph felt like unearthing a rare artifact. Because of its damning tone, jarringly dissonant from other scenes, I decided to reserve it for the Afterword rather than the main text. If my father were here today I suspect his first instinct would be to disavow these words, to say it was bullshit, that his parents were wonderful, and he was a weak ungrateful bastard for complaining about them. Tellingly, he never typed up this paragraph; literally and figuratively, he buried it.

During his decades-long obsessive quest to finish his memoir, I wonder if a part of my father didn't *want* to come to terms with his past. Maybe he was afraid the kindling fire of creativity could be extinguished by the quietness of 'closure.' Alcohol fueled both imagination and madness; he could in turn be wildly self-destructive or lash out at those he loved the most. Perhaps a fuller exploration of suppressed rage would have helped him be a healthier human being. But in *Boy on a Unicycle*, Dan McCall is his own harshest critic. He couldn't bear the thought of placing blame on his parents, he was convinced that was a coward's way out.

So he turned to drinking.
And writing.

ACKNOWLEDGMENTS

I am thankful to my father for writing this book and for my opportunity to share it. While editing, my most valuable ally and sounding board was the hero of "L'Envoi," Ms. Dorothy Kaufmann, whom I refer to more simply as "Mom." I appreciate the support from my wife Meg and the patience of my children, Evan and Ava. I am grateful for the encouragement and advice from many friends and colleagues, including Reuben Munday, Lamar Herrin, Chris Gallagher, Wayne Gladstone, Jon Roemer, Kathy Dewart, Andy Lobe, Kirsten Lobe, Kevin Murphy, Michael McCall, Glenn Altschuler, Sevan Terzian, Margaret Gallo, Edgar Rosenberg, Bill Friedlander, Betty Friedlander, Gerhard Joseph, Dan Wile, Alison Lurie, Rachel Dickinson, Amy Dickinson, Ed Zuckerman, and Philipp Meyer.

— Steven McCall

ABOUT DAN McCALL

Dan McCall (1940-2012) was the critically acclaimed author of ten books of fiction and nonfiction, including *Beecher* (Dutton Books), *Triphammer* (Atlantic Monthly Press), and *The Example of Richard Wright* (Harcourt Brace). Dan was also a Professor of Creative Writing and American Studies at Cornell University for forty years. His novel *Jack the Bear* (Doubleday), translated into a dozen languages, was made into a 20th Century Fox feature film.

CPSIA information can be obtained
at www.ICGtesting.com
Printed in the USA
BVOW03s1112130817
491837BV00039B/92/P